S0-BFA-591

REAL-WORLD MATHEMATICS THROUGH SCIENCE

INVESTIGATING APPLES

CHRISTINE V. JOHNSON

Nancy Cook, Project Director

Developed by Washington MESA

INNOVATIVE LEARNING PUBLICATIONS

 ADDISON-WESLEY PUBLISHING COMPANY

Menlo Park, California • Reading, Massachusetts • New York
Don Mills, Ontario • Wokingham, England • Amsterdam • Bonn
Paris • Milan • Madrid • Sydney • Singapore • Tokyo
Seoul • Taipei • Mexico City • San Juan

MESA wishes to express its appreciation to the following people for their advice and assistance, without which this module could not have been completed:

Nancy Cook, Ph.D.
Washington MESA
University of Washington
Seattle, Washington

Christine V. Johnson
Washington MESA
University of Washington
Seattle, Washington

John Baranowski, Ph.D.
Technical Services Manager
Tree Top, Inc.
Selah, Washington

Washington MESA middle-school mathematics and science teachers in Seattle, Spokane, Tacoma, Toppenish, and Yakima, Washington

Project Editor: Katarina Stenstedt
Production/Mfg. Coordinator: Leanne Collins
Design Manager: Jeff Kelly
Text Design: Michelle Taverniti
Cover Design: Dennis Teutschel
Cover Photograph: © 1995 Hank Delespinasse/The Image Bank

This book is published by Innovative Learning Publications™, an imprint of the Alternative Publishing Group of Addison-Wesley Publishing Company.

This material in part is based on work supported by Grant No. MDR–8751287 from the National Science Foundation; Instructional Materials Development; 1800 G Street NW; Washington, DC 20550. The material was designed and developed by Washington MESA (Mathematics, Engineering, Science Achievement); 353 Loew Hall FH-18; University of Washington; Seattle, WA 98195. Any opinions, findings, conclusions, or recommendations expressed in this publication are those of Washington MESA and do not necessarily reflect the views of the National Science Foundation.

ISBN 0–201–49040-4
2 3 4 5 6 7 8 9 10–DR–98 97 96 95 94

INVESTIGATING APPLES

Date Due

DE 1 '00			

BRODART, INC.   Cat. No. 23 233   Printed in U.S.A.

CONTENTS

INTRODUCTION

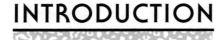

Investigating Apples is one of the middle-grades instructional modules created and field-tested by the Washington MESA (Mathematics, Engineering, Science Achievement) project. Washington MESA operates on the premise that effective classroom materials should facilitate connections between classroom and real-world mathematics and science. Staff members and teachers work with scientists, mathematicians, and engineers to outline each module. Pilot modules are tested in middle-school classrooms, then revised using feedback from the teachers.

The modules weave important mathematics themes with relevant, exciting science topics. The activities are based on current reform philosophies recommended by the National Council of Teachers of Mathematics' (NCTM's) *Curriculum and Evaluation Standards for School Mathematics* and the American Association for the Advancement of Science's *Project 2061*. Students will

◆ learn by doing. Students collect and analyze data on the masses, diameters, and heights of different varieties of apples, and they collect and analyze data from their family taste-test surveys.

◆ employ a variety of reasoning processes by using several ways to understand and present their data.

◆ learn to express technical concepts as they write and discuss answers to open-ended questions. The questions are designed to provoke further thought about how science and mathematics connect to the everyday world.

◆ learn the appropriate use of calculators by solving real problems. Students are taught how to conceptualize and set up problems that they can then solve using calculators.

◆ make connections between mathematics and science as well as within mathematics and science. Writing Link, History Link, Interest Link, and

Technology Link activities are included to expand the connections to other subject areas.

◆ explore careers through the Career Link features.

Investigating Apples directs middle-school students toward active involvement in learning. Students emulate real-world work environments by collaborating in small groups and striving for group consensus. They work with concrete materials and evaluate open-ended problems—the combination that helps the transition from concrete to abstract thinking crucial to the intellectual development of students at this age. To ascertain that instruction is working, assessment is integrated into *Investigating Apples* activities. Assessment and instruction goals are identical.

Family encouragement can help students to succeed educationally, so a special activity involves students' families in hands-on, collaborative work. Students learn as they show parents and other family members what they have learned.

Each activity begins with an Overview page summarizing what students will be doing and how the teacher needs to prepare. This is followed by background information for the teacher's use and a Presenting the Activity section, which describes the activity in detail and suggests discussion questions and assessment strategies. This is followed by Student Sheets and Transparency Masters in blackline master form. Some of the Student Sheets have answers that vary with the apple sample used, but where applicable, Completed Student Sheets are provided beginning on page 91. Career Link, History Link, Writing Link, Interest Link, and Technology Link features are found throughout the book.

CONCEPTUAL OVERVIEW

Investigating Apples addresses the following mathematics topics, science topics, and NCTM standards.

NCTM Curriculum Standards

Problem Solving
  Open-Ended
  Multiple Strategies
Communication
  Verbal and Written
Reasoning
  Logical and Spatial
  Predictions and Evaluations
Mathematical Connections
  Among Topics
  To Real-World Contexts

NCTM Teaching Standards

Worthwhile Tasks
  Real-World Contexts
Teacher's Role
  Listening and Observing
  Orchestrating Discourse
Enhancement Tools
  Calculators
  Concrete Materials
Learning Environment
  Collaborative Work

NCTM Evaluation Standards

Alignment
  Integral to Instruction
Multiple Sources
  Oral and Written
  Individual and Group
Multiple Methods
  Instructional Planning
  Grading
Mathematical Power
  Communicate
  Reason
  Integrate
  Generalize

Mathematics Content

Number Relationships
  Percents
Computation and Estimation
  Mental Arithmetic
  Calculators
  Numerical Estimation
Patterns and Functions
  Tables

Statistics
  Median
  Quartile
  Range
  Extremes
  Outliers
  Line Plot
  Stem Plot
  Box Plot
  Scatter Plot
  Associations
  Surveys
Measurement
  Metric
  Linear
  Mass

Science Topics

Pomology
  Growth Cycle
  Horticulture
  Food Science
Apple Sizing
  Mass
  Height
  Diameter
Scientific Process
  Observing
  Predicting
  Hypothesizing
  Analyzing
  Concluding

ACTIVITY OVERVIEW

Overview

Statistical concepts are becoming increasingly prominent in the middle-school mathematics curriculum. Students should develop an understanding of the concepts and processes used in analyzing data through relevant applications with possible connections to science and career opportunities.

Investigating Apples provides students with experiences collecting, organizing, representing, and interpreting data. The content, developed around the statistics used in the apple-growing industry, incorporates pomology and the careers of horticulturists, food scientists, and statisticians.

If you know a horticulturist, food scientist, or statistician who would be willing to visit the class, invite her or him to participate in some part of this module, so students can pursue their questions and ideas further.

Carefully explain the rules about safety. Although the knives and scissors used in some of the activities are common objects, they are sharp and students should use them with care.

Disposable latex gloves should not be reused, even if they appear to be still intact after one use. They are readily penetrated so that holes, though invisible, are likely to be present after even one use.

Except where specifically instructed in the Family Activity, students should not taste or eat anything that is handled in the activities. Because of the risk of inadvertent chemical poisoning, do not use any apparatus that is commonly associated with science laboratory work, such as a scale, balance, beaker, or graduated cylinder, even if the apparatus is brand new. Science labs are never suitable for the preparation of substances to be ingested, no matter how thoroughly one might think all hazards have been eliminated. Other precautions pertinent to different activities are described on the relevant pages.

Find out whether any students have health or allergy conditions that will affect their participation in activities that involve tasting and working with apples.

Activity 1: Nature's Balance

The students are introduced to pomology, the science of growing fruit, particularly apples. They discuss how the apple industry determines the relative size of an apple. They use balance beams to collect data on the masses of different varieties of apples that are considered to be the same size. Through measuring the masses of several dozen apples, they are confronted with the uncertainty of measurement and the need to organize the information. Preparing line plots representing the data for each variety of apple introduces the class to statistical displays.

Activity 2: Apple Stems

Students recognize and understand the importance of statistical reasoning as they continue to organize and interpret their data on the masses of apples in the same size category. They explore the stem plot as an additional method used by statisticians to display and analyze data. The work involved in apple production is presented as well as aspects of the career of a statistician.

Activity 3: Apple Boxes

Students continue to organize and interpret their data on the masses of apples while exploring the box plot, yet another method used to display and analyze data. Students compare the information gathered from all three types of plots to determine the advantages and disadvantages of each, as well as which technique they prefer. They are introduced to careers in pomology and begin to comprehend the responsibilities involved in the yearly cycle of apple cultivation and harvest.

Activity 4: Apple Statistics

Students further investigate questions relating to an apple's size as they collect data on the heights and diameters from each variety. They prepare and examine line plots, stem plots, and box plots to extend their experiences with preparing and interpreting statistical displays while assessing the effectiveness and uses of each plot. The role of statistics in improving and monitoring apple-storage procedures is presented.

Activity 5: New Relations

Students investigate the relation between height and mass and the relation between diameter and mass by constructing and analyzing scatter plots.

They analyze their plots and relate their findings to the process of sizing apples. In conclusion, the students investigate the connection between height and diameter.

Family Activity: Statistical Slices

Students are given an apple taste-test package containing portions of three varieties of apples. They conduct a survey and opinion poll with their families on the texture and flavor of each variety, rating them on a scale of 1 to 5. The collective data from the families are organized, displayed, and analyzed in class.

MATERIALS LIST

The following is a consolidated list of materials needed in *Investigating Apples*. A list of materials needed for each activity is included in the Overview for each activity.

Activity	Materials
Nature's Balance	*For the teacher:* ◆ Transparency Master 1.6 ◆ 2 or more apples of the same variety in different sizes *For each student:* ◆ Student Sheets 1.1–1.5, including multiple copies of 1.2 ◆ A pair of disposable latex gloves ◆ Calculator *For each group of students:* ◆ 1 dozen size-80 apples of a given variety ◆ Large plastic bag with closure tie ◆ Masking tape ◆ Balance
Apple Stems	*For the teacher:* ◆ A transparency of Student Sheet 2.2 *For each student:* ◆ Student Sheets 2.1–2.4 ◆ Extra copies of Student Sheet 2.2 ◆ Information from Student Sheets 1.3–1.5 ◆ A straightedge ◆ Scientific calculator
Apple Boxes	*For the teacher:* ◆ Transparency Master 3.4 ◆ A transparency of Student Sheet 3.2

Activity	Materials
	For each student: ◆ Student Sheets 3.1–3.3 ◆ Information from Student Sheets 2.1–2.4 ◆ A straightedge ◆ Scientific calculator *For each of the three groups:* ◆ A copy of Transparency Master 3.4
Apple Statistics	*For the teacher:* ◆ Transparency Master 4.5 ◆ 1 size-80 apple ◆ Kitchen paring knife *For the student* ◆ Student Sheets 4.1–4.4 ◆ Multiple copies of Student Sheet 4.2 ◆ A pair of disposable latex gloves ◆ Centimeter ruler *For each group of students* ◆ 2–3 kitchen paring knives ◆ 1 dozen apples in plastic bag from Activity 1 ◆ Masking tape and a cutting board
New Relations	*For the teacher:* ◆ A transparency of Student Sheet 5.2 *For the student:* ◆ Student Sheets 5.1–5.3 ◆ Multiple copies of Student Sheet 5.2 ◆ A straightedge
Family Activity	*For the teacher:* ◆ Transparency of Family Activity Sheet 5 *For each student:* ◆ Family Activity Sheets 1–6 ◆ 3–4 copies of Family Activity Sheet 2, depending on family size ◆ Family taste-test package prepared in Activity 4 *For each group of students:* ◆ Completed survey slips from one variety of apple

RESOURCES LIST

This list of resources was compiled by teachers, scientists, and professionals who participated in developing *Investigating Apples*. It is intended for teachers who would like to pursue the topic further with their class, with small groups of students who are particularly interested in the topic, with individual students who desire further investigations, or for their own professional development.

Apple Industry

Washington Apple Commission
P.O. Box 18
2900 Euclid Avenue
Wenatchee, WA 98807-0018
(509) 663-9600

Cooperative Extension
U.S. Department of Agriculture
Washington State University
Pullman, WA 99164-6230
(509) 664-5540

Apples Galore: History in Wenatchee
A. C. Bright
(good historical story about the
    beginning of apple processing in
    Washington state, pp. 235–245)

Tree Top, Inc.
P. O. Box 248
Selah, WA 98942-0248
(509) 697-7251

National Food Processors
    Association
1401 New York Ave. Northwest
Washington, DC 20005
(202) 639-5900

International Apple Institute
P. O. Box 1137
McLean, VA 22101
(703) 442-8850

Statistics

American Statistical Association
1429 Duke Street
Alexandria, VA 22314-3402
(703) 684-1221

Teaching Statistics

"Data Plots: Organizing and
  Representing Data"
Richard Thiessen
AIMS Newsletter
Vol. VI, No. 9, April 1992
pp. 6–8

Exploring Data
Quantitative Literacy Series
Landwehr and Watkins
Dale Seymour Publications
Palo Alto, CA 1987

*Exploring Surveys and Information
  from Samples*
Quantitative Literacy Series
Landwehr, Swift, Watkins
Dale Seymour Publications
Palo Alto, CA 1987

*From Home Runs to Housing Costs:
  Data Resource for Teaching
  Statistics*
Gail Burrill, editor
Dale Seymour Publications
Palo Alto, CA 1994

*Teaching Statistics: Guidelines for
  Elementary Through High School*
Center for Statistical Education,
American Statistical Association
Dale Seymour Publications
Palo Alto, CA 1994

On the Shoulders of Giants
Lyn Arthur Steen, Editor
National Academy Press
Washington, DC 1990

*Curriculum and Evaluation
  Standards*
National Council of Teachers of
  Mathematics
Reston, VA 1989, pp. 105–108

Dealing With Data and Chance
Curriculum and Evaluation
  Standards
Addenda Series, Grades 5–8
Judith Zawojewski
National Council of Teachers of
  Mathematics
Reston, VA 1991

*Student Poster Projects: Winners
  of the American Statistics Poster
  Competition, 1991–1992*
Center for Statistical Education,
American Statistical Association
Dale Seymour Publications
Palo Alto, CA 1994

ACTIVITY
1

NATURE'S BALANCE

Overview

This activity introduces pomology, the science of growing fruit, particularly apples. From information on the packing, sorting, and sizing of apples, students discuss questions on how the size of an apple is determined. They collect data on the masses of different varieties of size-80 apples and organize their data by preparing and analyzing a line plot.

Time. One or two 40- to 50-minute periods.

Purpose. Students begin to define statistics as the collection, organization, and interpretation of numerical data. Through collecting data on the masses of size-80 apples, they are confronted with the uncertainty of measurement and discover that the size of the data set can affect the outcome and the validity of their conclusions.

Materials. *For the teacher:*
◆ Transparency Master 1.6
◆ 2 or more apples of the same variety in different sizes

For each student:
◆ Student Sheets 1.1–1.5, including multiple copies of 1.2
◆ A pair of disposable latex gloves
◆ Calculator

For each group of students:
◆ 1 dozen size 80-apples of a given variety
◆ Large plastic bag with closure tie
◆ Masking tape
◆ Balance

Getting Ready
1. Acquire nine dozen size-80 apples, three dozen of three varieties.
2. Divide the class into thirds. Each third will collect data on a different variety of size-80 apples. Divide each third into three groups so they can work with one dozen apples per group.
3. Duplicate Student Sheets 1.1–1.5, including multiple copies of 1.2.
4. Prepare Transparency Master 1.6.
5. Locate masking tape, disposable gloves, plastic bags, and balances.

Background Information

After being harvested, apples are sorted by size and packed in fiberboard cartons for shipment. Each box contains 42 pounds of fruit, packed by count. For example, a size 100 box has 100 apples of equal size for a combined weight of 42 pounds. Other standard pack sizes range from 48 (a very large piece of fruit with limited supply) to 216. Sizes 48 through 80 are considered large apples, 88 through 125 are medium apples, and 138 through 214 are small apples. The chart below gives approximate masses of different sizes of apples.

Scale of Size and Approximate Mass

Size	Mass in Grams	Size	Mass in Grams
48	397	125	153
56	340	138	136
64	298	150	127
72	264	163	116
80	238	175	108
88	215	198	96
100	190	216	88
113	167		

Each activity in this module refers to size 80-apples, which reinforces the concept of uniform size. If your apples are sized differently, adjust accordingly. Write to an apple producer or ask your local grocer about buying apples in bulk.

In this activity, students are introduced to statistics as they collect data on the masses of apples in the same size category. They begin to understand the uncertainty of measurement as they prepare a line plot to represent their data.

Line plots are a quick and simple way to organize data. From a line plot it is easy to spot the largest and smallest values, outliers, clusters, and gaps in the data. It gives a clear presentation of the distribution and a method for determining the median mass. As an example, the following set of line plots represents the mass data collected for three varieties of apples. Each sample contains 36 size-80 apples.

Line Plots for the Mass of size-80 Apples

Red Delicious
Median Mass = 237.5

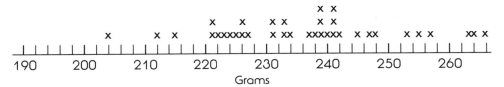

Granny Smith
Median Mass = 220

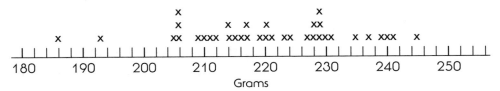

Rome Beauty
Median Mass = 212.5

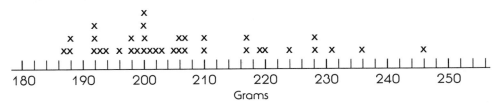

Many procedures in this module involve the median, or middle value, in a set of numbers, rather than the mean. There are two reasons for this. First, the median is a simpler idea and requires less computation. Second, the median is not affected by a few extremely large or small values as is the mean. For these reasons, statisticians often prefer the median in data analysis.

Throughout each activity in this unit, students are asked their opinion and to describe what they observe about their data. Writing interpretations of statistical data is an important communication skill. In order to encourage students to become comfortable with this expectation, emphasize that there are no correct answers or responses. Their individual ideas matter.

Presenting The Activity

Apple Sizes. Discuss with the students how they would find apples of many different sizes growing on an apple tree; yet when they purchase them in a store, the apples displayed appear to be exactly the same size. Bags of apples also seem to contain apples of the same size, though often smaller than bulk apples. Ask the students:

◆ Why do you think this uniformity occurs?

Refer to the Interest Links "Pomology" and "The Harvest." If possible, show them two sizes of apples from the same variety for comparison. Then ask the following question and list their suggestions:

◆ How do you think the size of an apple is determined?

Refer to the background information to interpret the apple industry's method of assigning a size value to an apple. For example, a size-80 apple means that 80 apples of that size will fill a 42-pound box.

Mass. Display Transparency Master 1.6. It gives the approximate masses for various sizes of apples. Ask:

◆ Is every size-80 Red Delicious apple exactly the same?

Show students several size-80 apples of the same variety and ask:

◆ Do they look the same?

◆ Are size-80 apples of different varieties exactly the same? Present several size-80 samples of three varieties for them to compare visually.

◆ If not, how do they vary?

◆ Why isn't there a size-75 apple?

◆ Could an apple's mass equal 200 grams? If so, what size apple is it? How do you know?

What Is Statistics? Define statistics as a branch of mathematics that involves collecting, organizing, describing, representing, and interpreting numerical data. The techniques of statistics provide powerful tools for managing collections of data and helping to answer questions about the data. Tell students that in this activity they will collect data on the masses of size-80 apples and begin to answer questions about the relative sizes of apples.

Give each student a pair of disposable latex gloves to wear for sanitation purposes. Divide the class into thirds. Distribute three dozen size-80 apples of one variety to a third of the class. Divide each third into three groups, and give them one dozen apples, masking tape, and a balance beam to collect their initial mass data. Before beginning, have the groups decide which group will number their apples 1–12, which group will number their apples 13–24, and which group will number their apples 25–36.

Apple Masses. Hand out Student Sheets 1.1 and 1.2. As the students work on question 10, check to see that they understand the process for preparing a line plot. After students have collected their data and completed both pages of Student Sheet 1.1, the apples should be placed in a plastic bag, sealed, labeled with their apple variety and select numbers, then stored in a refrigerator that is used only for storing food. (Do not use a refrigerator used for storing nonedible materials such as chemicals and biology experiments.) Other equipment may also be put away at this time.

Tell students they will often be asked to describe what they have learned or observed by looking at the data. They are to write down any observations they make and any questions that occur to them. There are no right answers. The ability to organize, summarize, and communicate numerical information is a necessary skill in mathematics and science.

Explain that they are going to enlarge their sample to include the data from the other groups measuring the same variety of apple.

Seeds for Thought. Pass out all three pages of Student Sheet 1.3. Arrange the class in thirds based on the variety of apples on which they collected data. Suggest that select students read the masses of apples 1–12, 13–24, and 25–36 while everyone in the group records the information into their table. Each student should now complete Student Sheet 1.3. In order to incorporate the additional mass data onto their existing line plot, students may find that they must extend their number line in either direction.

When they have finished Student Sheet 1.3 and discussed the results within their small groups, they should begin work on Student Sheets 1.4 and 1.5, activities that provide further experience with line plots. Each of these student sheets provides space to collect the mass data on another variety of apples. If time is a factor, the data can be collected in class from the students who measured the apples, and the line plots completed as homework.

Discussion Questions

1. What are the median masses for the different varieties of apples in the class?

2. Are the data you have collected reliable?

3. Have the data been collected in a reasonable manner?

4. What is the significance of outliers?

5. Does the table of size and mass match your data results?

Assessment Questions

1. Find the mean mass for your variety and size of apple. How does the mean mass compare to the median mass and your estimated average? Does an extreme mass cause a greater change in the mean or the median? Which average do you prefer for your data and why?

2. Give the mass of four different apples whose median mass is 200 grams, but whose average mass is 165 grams.

3. Find and describe any mathematical patterns you see in the size and mass table for various sizes of apples.

The Harvest

The apple crop is harvested in the fall when the apples are fully grown and ripened. Decades ago, the perfect time to harvest was based on weather, crop condition, and by tasting the apple for crispness and sweetness. Today, the decision is less art and more science. Scientific tests are used to gauge fruit firmness, sugar-solid level, and color.

Most of the crop is picked from the trees by hand. The best apples are washed and sorted by size. Trees do not grow only one size of fruit—the location of the apple on the tree, how much sunlight it gets, irrigation practices, how the tree was thinned, and other factors make the apples different sizes. As apples arrive at the packing house, they are initially sorted by optical scanner and human hands into three or four grades based on color, shape, firmness, and sugar-solid content. Then within each of these grades, the apples are sorted into as many as fifteen size categories.

Cull apples, unsuitable for the fresh market, make up ten to fifteen percent of the harvest. They are usually sent to a processing plant. In all, nearly half of the apple crop grown ends up processed into canned, frozen, or dehydrated apple products such as applesauce, apple juice or cider, apple butter, and apple slices.

The apples are packed and delivered by refrigerated trains and trucks to markets and grocery stores. Some apples are stored in special, air-tight coolers which keep the apples from rotting. Months after the harvest season is over, you can find these apples, still fresh, on the shelf in your store.

Pomology

Those colorful, well-flavored apples piled up in the produce sections of the grocery store didn't grow entirely without help. They are the result of years of scientific research. There's even a name for the science of growing apples and other fruits—*pomology* (pō-mol-e-jee). Pomology deals with fertilization, pruning, insect and disease control, fruit thinning, harvesting, and storage techniques. A description of how pomology helps the apples get from the field to the store to your mouth follows.

An apple tree needs four to five years to produce its first fruits. It will continue producing apples until a peak age of thirty-five to forty years. But there are some trees nearly two hundred years old that still produce apples! The apple varieties we munch on don't come from a seed. Through a process called *grafting,* farmers tape or tie live buds from old trees of the desired variety to a slit in a growing seedling. Then the seedling can grow to produce the old tree's variety of apple. Grafting trees has perpetuated apple varieties for hundreds of years.

The first and most important decision of a fruit grower is what variety to plant. Since the success or failure of the crop depends on this, growers and pomologists spend a lot of time testing apple varieties and studying how they will grow in different areas. How many varieties are there? In all, 7,000 varieties of apples have been named. There are 2,500 varieties grown in the United States, only 100 commercially. Of these, the top ten are: Red Delicious, Golden Delicious, Granny Smith, McIntosh, York Imperial, Rome Beauty, Jonathan, Stayman, Newtown Pippin, and Winesap.

Apple Masses

1. My group is one of three groups collecting data on size _____ _____
   apples.
   (#)   (variety of apple)

2. There are _____ apples in the three groups, and _____ apples in my group's
   sample.   (#)   (#)

3. The apples are to be numbered. Among the three groups decide which numbers each group will use. The apples in my group's sample will be numbered:

   A. 1–12   B. 13–24   C. 25–36

4. Use masking tape and label each apple in your sample with an appropriate
   number.

5. List the numbers of your apples in the
   left-hand column of the table.

6. If any of your apples have stems,
   remove them.

7. Use the balance to measure the mass
   of each apple in your sample to the
   nearest gram. Record the results in the
   table.

8. According to your sample, a

   _____ apple's mass is

   between _____ and _____ grams.

9. Line up your 12 apples in order from
   smallest to largest. What do you see?

Apple Data	
Number	Mass

10. Put your apples in a plastic bag. Label it and give it to your teacher.

11. A line plot is a quick way to organize and visualize your data. Use Student Sheet 1.2 and follow these steps to prepare a line plot representing the mass of apples in your sample.

    Turn your graph paper sideways and draw a horizontal line near the bottom edge.

    Put a number scale on this line. Since the smallest apple in your sample is

    _____ grams, and the largest is _____ grams, your scale should include these numbers.

    Plot your apple data by marking an "x" above the line at the appropriate mass.

    If more than one apple has the same mass, put the additional points one unit above the other, stacking them on the graph.

12. Describe what you observe about the masses of apples from your line plot.

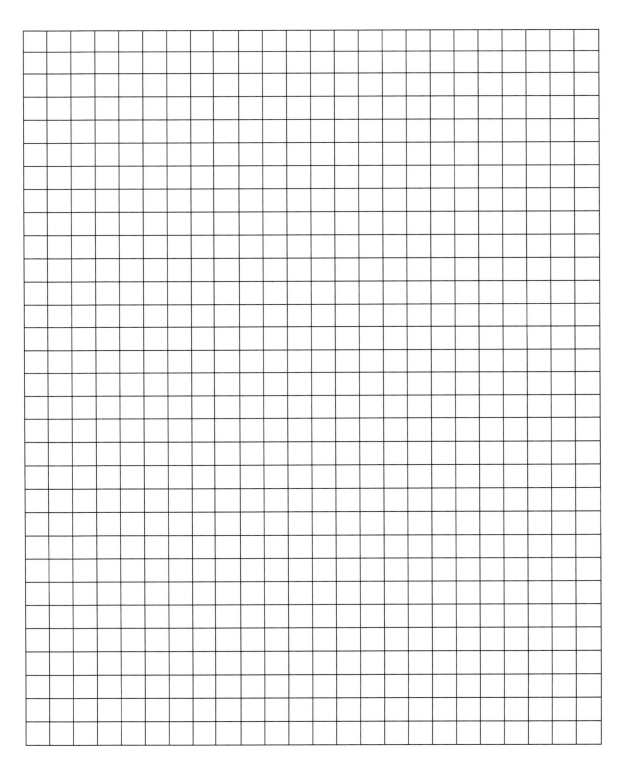

Seeds for Thought

1. Enlarge your sample size by collecting data from the other two groups in your class measuring the same variety of apple. Record the information in the table below.

Mass of _____ Apples
      (apple variety)

Number	Mass	Number	Mass	Number	Mass
1		13		25	
2		14		26	
3		15		27	
4		16		28	
5		17		29	
6		18		30	
7		19		31	
8		20		32	
9		21		33	
10		22		34	
11		23		35	
12		24		36	

2. Add the mass for each new apple to your line plot. Be careful not to replot your original 12 apples. Before beginning, you might want to check off the numbers for apples you have already placed on the graph.

   There should be _____ points on your line plot. Are there?

3. Is the range for all 36 apples different from the range of your original 12 apples? Explain. Use a separate piece of paper if you need to.

4. All these apples are considered the same size. Do you think they are the same size? Explain.

5. Do you think that there exists an apple in this variety and size category that has a mass 20 grams less than your smallest apple or 20 grams more than your largest apple? Why, or why not?

6. According to the data for all 36 apples, the size _____ _____

                                                          (#)   (variety)

apple has a mass between _____ and _____ grams.

7. A line plot often emphasizes features of the data that were not apparent from the list. These include:

Outliers: Data values that are very much larger or smaller than the other values.
Clusters: Isolated groups of points.
Gaps: Large spaces between points.

   a. The masses of which apples, if any, appear to be outliers?

   b. Do the data seem to fall into clusters on the line plot? If so, where?

   c. Are there any gaps in the data? If so, where?

8. The median mass is the mass exactly in the middle of the range.

   a. Use your line plot to find the median apple mass for your variety of apple.

   b. Describe how you determined the median mass.

9. What percent of your apples have a mass less than the median mass?

   _____

10. What percent have a mass more than the median mass? _____

11. Write a brief description of the information displayed in the line plot.

Food for Thought

1. Obtain data from a group in your class measuring a second variety of apple. Record the information in the table below.

Mass of _____ Apples
        (apple variety)

Number	Mass	Number	Mass	Number	Mass
1		13		25	
2		14		26	
3		15		27	
4		16		28	
5		17		29	
6		18		30	
7		19		31	
8		20		32	
9		21		33	
10		22		34	
11		23		35	
12		24		36	

2. Make a line plot of the data.

3. Is the range for these 36 apples different from the range of your original 36 apples? Explain.

4. The size _____ _____ apple has a mass between _____ and
         (#)   (variety)

   _____ grams.

5. Are there any outliers in the data? If so, where?

6. Does the data seem to fall into clusters on the line plot? If so, where?

7. Are there any gaps in the data? If so, where?

8. Calculate the median mass for this variety of apple.

9. How does the median mass of these apples compare to the median mass of
   the first variety? Explain.

Further Food for Thought

1. Obtain data from a group in your class measuring a third variety of apple. Record the information in the table below.

Mass of _____ Apples
         (apple variety)

Number	Mass	Number	Mass	Number	Mass
1		13		25	
2		14		26	
3		15		27	
4		16		28	
5		17		29	
6		18		30	
7		19		31	
8		20		32	
9		21		33	
10		22		34	
11		23		35	
12		24		36	

2. Make a line plot of the data.

3. Is the range in this sample different from the range in either of the other samples? Explain.

4. The size _____ _____ apple has a mass between _____ and
          (#)   (variety)

   _____ grams.

5. Are there any outliers in the data? If so, where?

6. Does the data seem to fall into clusters on the line plot? If so, where?

7. Are there any gaps in the data? If so, where?

8. Calculate the median apple mass for this variety of apple.

9. How does the median mass of these apples compare to the median mass of
   the two other varieties? Explain.

The Size of Apples

Size	Mass in Grams
48	397
56	340
64	298
72	264
80	238
88	215
100	190
113	167
125	153
138	136
150	127
163	116
175	108
198	96
216	88

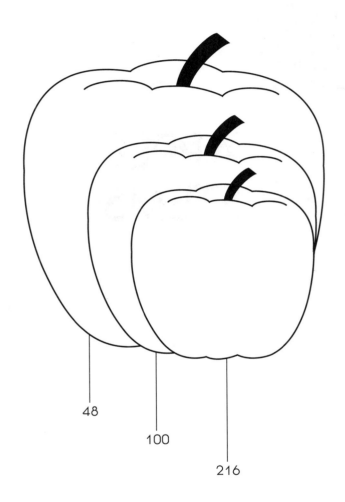

48

100

216

ACTIVITY
2

APPLE
STEMS

Overview

Students continue to organize and interpret their data on the mass of size-80 apples while exploring the stem plot, which is another method used by statisticians to display and analyze data. They are introduced to the career of a statistician and begin to comprehend the wide range of opportunities in this field.

Time. One or two 40- to 50-minute class periods.

Purpose. Students recognize and understand the importance of statistical reasoning. They learn of multiple ways to display the same data, and that each way has its advantages.

Materials. *For the teacher:*

◆ A transparency of Student Sheet 2.2

For each student:

◆ Student Sheets 2.1–2.4

◆ Extra copies of Student Sheet 2.2

◆ Information from Student Sheets 1.3–1.5

◆ A straightedge

◆ Scientific calculator

Getting Ready

1. Duplicate Student Sheets 2.1–2.4, including duplicate copies of Student Sheet 2.2.

2. Prepare a transparency of Student Sheet 2.2.

3. Locate calculators and straightedges.

Background Information

Often more than one method is used to display and interpret a set of data. This activity explores another way to display the mass data from Activity 1, providing a different perspective with useful and interesting information about the data.

A line plot tends to have a sizable spread that can make it difficult to recognize patterns, and the presentation may be less effective as a tool to aid in interpreting the data. The stem plot provides an alternative method to organize and present data by grouping it into intervals. Statisticians use a stem plot as a substitute for histograms and bar graphs because it is easier to construct and all the original data values are displayed.

These stem plots represent the same mass data used to prepare the line plots in the Background of Activity 1 (page 3). The vertical column of numbers is called the stem, and the numbers to the right are referred to as the leaves.

Red Delicious

20 | 4 represents
204 grams

18	
19	
20	4
21	2 5
22	1 1 2 3 4 5 6 6 7
23	1 1 3 3 4 7 8 9 9 9
24	0 1 1 1 2 5 7 8
25	3 5 7
26	3 4 6
27	

Granny Smith

18 | 6 represents
186 grams

18	6
19	3
20	5 6 6 6 9
21	0 1 2 4 4 5 6 7 7 9
22	0 0 1 3 4 7 8 8 9 9 9
23	0 1 5 7 9
24	0 1 5
25	
26	

Rome Beauty

```
19 | 7 represents        18 | 7 8 8
197 grams               19 | 2 2 2 3 4 6 8 8 9
                        20 | 0 0 0 0 1 2 3 5 6 6 7 7
                        21 | 0 0 7 7 9
                        22 | 0 4 8 8
                        23 | 1 6
                        24 | 6
                        25 |
                        26 |
```

The numbers in the stems are the hundreds and tens places of each of the data values while the leaves are the numbers in the ones places of the data entries. For example, the data value 197 grams is represented in the plot as a 19 in the stem and a 7 as a leaf. The mass of 200 grams occurs four times in the Rome Beauty mass data and is represented in the plot as a 20 in the stem and four zeros as leaves to the right of the stem.

The stem plot shows the shape of the data more clearly than the line plot. The fairly symmetrical bell-shaped distribution with the lows balancing the highs is a common shape.

Stem plots offer a convenient way to directly compare two sets of grouped data. Use the same stem for both sets of data and place the leaves for one set to the right of the stem and the other set of leaves to the left of the stem. This is often referred to as a back-to-back stem plot.

```
      Red Delicious  |    | Granny Smith
                     | 18 | 6
                     | 19 | 3
                   4 | 20 | 5 6 6 6 9
                 5 2 | 21 | 0 1 2 4 4 5 6 7 7 9
         7 6 6 5 4 3 2 1 1 | 22 | 0 0 1 3 4 7 8 8 9 9 9
       9 9 9 8 7 4 3 3 1 1 | 23 | 0 1 5 7 9
         8 7 5 2 1 1 1 0 | 24 | 0 1 5
                 7 5 3 | 25 |
                 6 4 3 | 26 |
```

The basic aspects to be described numerically about a set of data are the center of the distribution and the spread of the distribution. There are two common sets of descriptive measures for location and spread: the median with the range, or the mean with standard deviation. Determining the median and the range requires only counting and an understanding of simple fractions: $\frac{1}{4}$, $\frac{1}{2}$, and $\frac{3}{4}$. Because they are easier to calculate, comprehend, and interpret than the more sophisticated standard deviation, the median and range are sometimes the preferred measures.

Line plots and stem plots both have a worthwhile role for exploring the sets of mass data collected on size-80 apples.

Presenting the Activity

Statisticians. Explain to students that statistics, in its simplest form, is a science that arranges many facts into an organized picture of the data. Within the arrangement, numbers ordered from the smallest to the largest are sometimes clustered in reasonable intervals, and patterns become apparent.

Statisticians may need to determine which number occurs most frequently, what is the average of all the numbers, which number is in the middle, or how great is the span from the largest to the smallest number. They make certain charts and plot the numbers on graph paper. They may also compare one set of numbers to another to discover the similarities and the differences. Each number in the data is significant and represents something important. A statistician determines the best way to organize the numbers to produce useful information for solving problems and making predictions. Refer to the Career Link for more information on statisticians.

Inform students that through this activity they will explore another type of statistical plot—the stem plot. Comparisons between the stem plot and the line plot display will be made as they continue to analyze the data that has been collected on the mass of apples.

Apple Stems. Divide the class into the same groups as used in Activity 1. Using a transparency of Student Sheet 2.2 and referring to question 1 on the first page of Student Sheet 2.1, introduce and clarify the process for creating a stem plot. Suggest that students put the leaves on in the order that the mass values appear in their table on Student Sheet 1.3. They should not try to find all the values that go on the first stem, then all the values that go on the second stem, and so forth. To put the leaves in order, quickly make a second plot next to the first one on the same sheet of graph paper. Tell students that each leaf value should take up the same amount of space, one square on the graph paper.

Distribute Student Sheets 2.1 and 2.2, calculators, and if necessary, Student Sheet 1.3. When the class has completed their stem plots and sufficiently answered the questions, conduct a discussion on their responses to questions 3–5. When students describe the shape of the data in question 3, encourage them to look for symmetry, single or multiple peaks, and amount of spread about the center.

Hand out both pages of Student Sheet 2.3, and have the students, working in their groups, make a stem plot for the data from Student Sheet 1.4. Student Sheet 2.4 provides space for making a stem plot of the data from Student Sheet 1.5, and can be done as homework.

Discussion Questions

1. Why is the median referred to as a type of average?

2. What does the range tell you?

3. What are the advantages of having the mass data information in the form of a graph?

4. Which type of plot do you prefer? Explain.

5. Can you think of situations where you might prefer one type of plot over another?

6. Is there a mass value that appears most often in your data?

Assessment Questions

1. Work with someone from another group to prepare a back-to-back stem plot that compares the mass values of two varieties of apples.

2. Construct a single stem plot that represents the combined mass data of all the apple varieties in the class. Write a paragraph summarizing the results.

3. If I tell you that I have a Granny Smith apple with a mass of 100 grams, what conclusions can you make about my apple?

Statisticians

Statisticians analyze the world. There are statisticians at work in practically every field—agriculture, economics, psychology, education, public health, physics, and engineering, just to name a few. What do they do for these fields? They investigate numbers. Numbers can reveal trends, averages, increases, and patterns. Statisticians collect the numbers (data), analyze them, and draw conclusions. They may forecast population growth or economic conditions, estimate crop yield, predict and evaluate the result of a new marketing program, or help engineers and scientists determine the best design for a jet airplane.

Statistics is a job for the curious, objective, and patient. Would you like to find out how long, on average, it takes a student to use up a pencil eraser? That's statistics. Or how many bald eagles live on the Pacific Coast? That's statistics too. Statisticians

◆ Collect data
◆ Make sure the method for collecting data is accurate and complete
◆ Analyze the data
◆ Make recommendations based on the strengths and limitations of the results

To pursue a career as a statistician, take all the mathematics, science, and computer courses you can. You need mathematics to understand the language and theory of statistics. The computer is not only used for calculations, but also to communicate through words and graphics. Statisticians work cooperatively with others, so it is important to develop good oral and written communication skills.

As science and technology make our world more complex, statistical reasoning becomes increasingly important. New opportunities for statisticians are constantly appearing in areas such as law, public policy, environmental science, and management. For at least the next decade there will be more positions open for statisticians than there will be applicants with appropriate training.

Apple Facts

◆ Apple growing is an important industry in the United States. The annual crop of about 200 million bushels comes mainly from 35 states with the right climates for apple growing.

◆ The state of Washington produces almost half the apples grown in the United States, 75 million bushels, followed by New York at 25 million, and Michigan at 20 million. One bushel yields 42 pounds of apples.

◆ How about a dozen long-stemmed red apples? Apples are members of the rose family, along with strawberries, almonds, and apricots.

◆ Apples are one of the oldest and most widely grown fruits.

◆ There are more than 15,000 commercial apple growers in the United States. The average orchard is 35 acres, but some cover as many as 3,000 acres. Trees are planted 27 to 500 per acre depending on the size of the tree at maturity. Efficient management brings crop yields of 1,000 to 2,000 bushels per acre.

◆ A red apple won't turn red without the sun. Sunlight causes chemical reactions in the apple's skin, making it produce a red coloring. Apple growers prune their trees into pyramid shapes so the sunlight can reach the lower branches and apples.

◆ Statistics is important to the apple industry. When agricultural scientists experiment with irrigation methods, they use statistics to improve the accuracy of their conclusions. In the apple-packing houses, statisticians chart the grade and size distribution over the years for a particular apple orchard. They use this information to predict what apple sizes and grades they can expect from a given region. Fruit is selected and picked in various sizes and stages of ripeness from individual orchards to study the effects of regular and controlled-atmosphere storage. The results from these samples help growers determine the best time for harvesting apples in an area.

Apple Stems

1. A stem plot gives another picture of the mass distribution for your size

   _____ _____ apples. Follow the directions below to construct a stem
   (#)   (variety)
   plot for the data on Student Sheet 1.3.

   a. List the smallest and largest values that you recorded to the nearest gram.

      Smallest _____   Largest _____

   b. Determine the stem values by eliminating the ones digits from both the
      smallest mass and largest mass recorded. (The stem value for the number

      176 would be 17.) Your stem will be the numbers from _____ to _____.

   c. On graph paper (Student Sheet 2.2) list your stem numbers vertically with a
      line to their right, similar to example (A) below.

   d. Place the ones digit from each mass entry to the right of the appropriate
      stem. These become the leaves. Example (B) below shows how 176, 189,
      183, and 200 grams would be listed.

   e. Arrange the leaves on a new plot so that they are in order from smallest to
      largest as in example (C).

   f. Add the explanation to the left of your plot as in (D).

A. 17		B. 17	6		C. 17	6		D.		17	6
18		18	9 3		18	3 9		17 | 6		18	3 9
19		19			19			represents		19	
20		20	0		20	0		176 grams		20	0

2. According to your stem plot, most of the apples have masses in the

   _____ s.

3. Rotate your stem plot 90 degrees counterclockwise. Describe the shape of
   the data.

4. On a separate sheet of paper, write a one-paragraph summary of the data displayed in the stem plot. Look for and describe patterns in the distribution of the data. Include discussion on outliers, clusters, gaps, and the location of the median.

5. Do the line and stem plots show any different information? Explain.

Which is easier to interpret? Why?

Which do you prefer? Why?

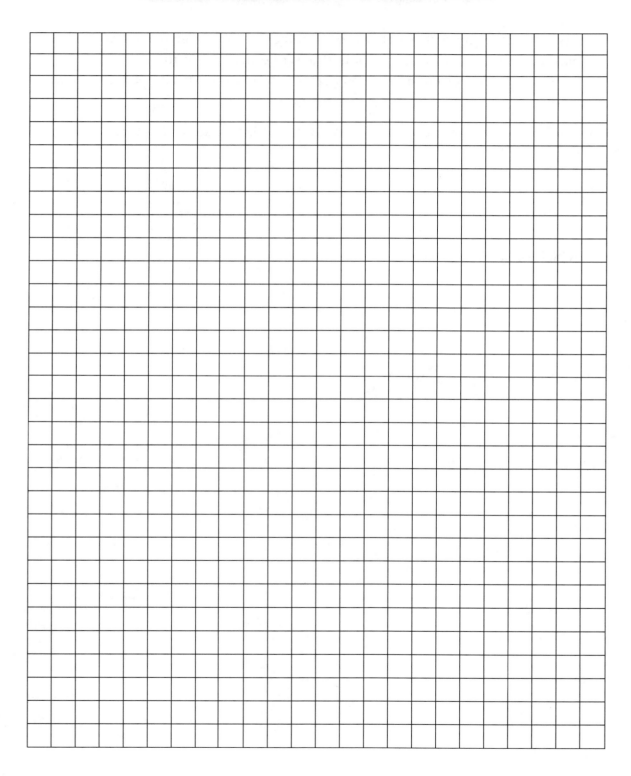

Stem Plots

1. Using the data on Student Sheet 1.4, construct a stem plot of the mass distribu-

   tion for size _____ _____ apples.
                  (#)   (variety)

2. According to your stem plot, most of the apples have masses in the

   _____s.

3. How does the mass of a size _____ _____ apple compare to the
                              (#)   (variety)

   mass of a size _____ _____ apple from Student Sheet 1.3? Explain.
                (#)   (variety)

4. Rotate your stem plot 90 degrees counterclockwise. Describe the shape of
   the data.

5. Write a one-paragraph summary of the data displayed in the stem plot. Look for and describe patterns in the distribution of the data. Include discussion on outliers, clusters, gaps, and the location of the median.

6. How does the mass distribution for these two varieties of apples compare? Examine the line plots for these two varieties of apples, and then the stem plots. Does one of these methods of plotting the data, line plots or stem plots, make this comparison more easy or more understandable? Explain.

Stem Comparisons

1. Using the data on Student Sheet 1.5, construct a stem plot of the mass

    distribution for size _____ _____ apples.
                      (#)   (variety)

2. According to your stem plot, most of the apples have masses in the

    _____s.

3. How do the masses of these three varieties of apple compare:

(size)	(variety)	(median mass)	(range of mass)
(size)	(variety)	(median mass)	(range of mass)
(size)	(variety)	(median mass)	(range of mass)

4. Examine each of the three stem plots. Compare and contrast the patterns for outliers, clusters, and gaps. Write a one-paragraph discussion regarding apple size and mass.

APPLE
BOXES

Overview

Students continue to organize and interpret their data on the masses of size-80 apples while exploring the box plot, yet another method used by statisticians to display and analyze data. Students compare the information gathered from all three types of plots to determine the advantages and disadvantages of each, as well as which technique they prefer. They are introduced to careers in pomology and begin to comprehend the yearly cycle of apple cultivation and harvest.

Time. One or two 40- to 50-minute class periods.

Purpose. Students continue to recognize and understand the importance of statistical reasoning. They realize how the apple industry relies on statistics to enhance production and to appropriately utilize technological developments. They learn that each type of statistical display is worthwhile for exploring a set of data.

Materials. *For the teacher:*
◆ Transparency Master 3.4
◆ A transparency of Student Sheet 3.2

For each student:
◆ Student Sheets 3.1–3.3
◆ Information from Student Sheets 2.1–2.4
◆ A straightedge
◆ Scientific calculator

For each of the three groups:
◆ A copy of Transparency Master 3.4

Getting Ready
1. Duplicate Student Sheets 3.1–3.3.
2. Prepare Transparency Master 3.4.
3. Make copies of Transparency Master 3.4.
4. Locate calculators and straightedges.

Background Information

Students have made and analyzed both line plots and stem plots. They have discovered that the basic aspects to be described numerically about a set of data are the center of the distribution and the spread of the distribution. They have been introduced to one common set of descriptive measures for central location and spread: the median and the range. In this activity, they are introduced to a new measure of spread, the quartile. Determining the median and the quartiles requires only counting and understanding the simple fractions $\frac{1}{4}$, $\frac{1}{2}$, and $\frac{3}{4}$. Since the median and quartiles are easy to calculate, comprehend, and interpret, they are frequently the preferred measures.

The stem plot can be used to find the median and quartiles of a set of data. The lower quartile is the median of the set of values below the median of the entire set of data. The upper quartile is the median of the values above the median of the set of data.

For the 36 size-80 Red Delicious apples whose masses are displayed in the stem plot in Activity 2 (page 22), the median mass is 237.5 grams, the lower quartile is 225.5 grams, and the upper quartile is 242.5 grams. The difference between the two quartiles gives the interquartile range (IQR); in this example the IQR is 17 grams. These simple measures and the smallest and largest values lead to a useful display called the box plot.

A box plot consists of a rectangular box that extends from the lower quartile to the upper quartile of the data and two lines (whiskers) that extend from the ends of the box to the extreme values.

Box Plot Displays of the Mass Data from Page 22

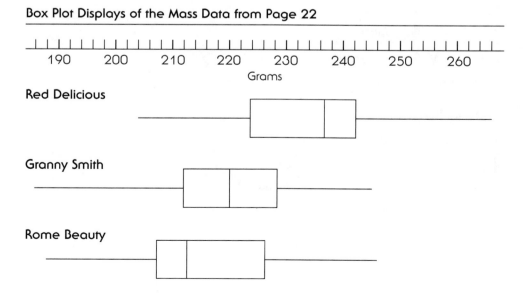

The box plot is more difficult to make, but it is useful in comparing several sets of data because it highlights only a few important features. The disadvantage is that once it is constructed, specific data values can no longer be read from it except for the median, the quartiles, and the extremes. Clusters and gaps are no longer apparent, nor is the shape of the distribution evident. The box plot is a summary display since it shows only certain statistics, not all the data.

Line plots, stem plots, and box plots each have a different, but worthwhile, role in helping students explore the sets of mass data collected on size-80 apples.

Presenting the Activity

Give each group a copy of Transparency Master 3.4 as a way to introduce the idea of a box plot display. Transparency Master 3.4 gives a month-to-month management chart used in the apple industry. The Career Link on apple growers explains in more detail the apple grower's month-to-month duties. Ask students the following questions:

◆ What does the chart show?

◆ How does it indicate time?

◆ How was the chart made?

◆ How accurate is the chart?

Boxing Apples. Remind students that they calculated the median mass for their particular variety of apple in Activity 1. Ask:

◆ What is meant by the median mass?

◆ How might it be determined?

Tell them that the median is a type of average. The median mass along with several other key points in the distribution will be used to prepare a box plot display of the apple mass data.

Hand out Student Sheets 3.1–3.2 and straightedges. Point out to students that this activity will take them through the process of accurately listing the mass values of their apples in order from least to greatest while dividing the data into four equivalent groups. From this list, they will determine their lower quartile, which is numerically halfway between the smallest mass value and the median; as well as their upper quartile, which is numerically halfway between the median and largest mass value.

Instruct students to complete the first page of Student Sheet 3.1 and discuss the solutions within their group before continuing on to the second page. They should then follow the steps to develop their box plot display, compare results within their groups, and finish answering the questions on the second and third pages.

The mass data on Transparency Master 1.6 may be used to demonstrate the process for preparing a box plot.

Spend time developing and analyzing question 6. The dramatic difference in appearance between the stem plot and the box plot ought to provide some interesting points for a class discussion on question 9. In conclusion, remind them that the box plot makes it easier to focus attention on the median, extremes, and quartiles and comparisons among groups.

Mention that box plots below the same number line are the best way to compare several sets of data. Ask:

◆ How would the mass data box plots for each apple variety in the class compare?

◆ Would they be similar, or considerably different?

Determine the basis for their hypotheses.

Solicit from students the information they would need in order to construct box plots representing the mass data for other varieties of apples in the class. After they have determined the five points required, inform them that they will make box plots of the mass data for the other varieties of apples on the same graph paper as their existing box plot in order to compare the three varieties of apples.

Branching Out. Distribute both pages of Student Sheet 3.3. Suggest that each student complete question 1 by recording the necessary information from the class discussion. The remainder of this activity can be finished as homework to allow adequate time for responding to the questions. Stress the importance of writing thoughtful and complete comments about the characteristics of the data, and that there are no right and wrong answers to many of the questions.

Have select students or volunteers put the different box plots on a transparency of Student Sheet 3.2 to promote class discussion relating to questions 3–8.

The History Link "Rachel Carson" can be used at any time to spark student interest.

Discussion Questions

1. What are the advantages and disadvantages of a box plot compared to a line plot?
2. What does the interquartile range tell you?
3. Is the interquartile range $\frac{1}{2}$ of the range of the distribution?
4. Are the whiskers always the same length? What do they tell you?

Assessment Questions

1. Describe what each aspect of a box plot tells you about the data.
2. Construct a single box plot that represents the combined mass data of all the apple varieties in the class. Write a paragraph summarizing the results.
3. Describe a situation where you would prefer a box plot rather than a line or stem plot. Explain why.

Apple Growers

The endless cycle of apple cultivation and harvest keeps pomologists and apple growers busy all year. The average grower tends to 6,650 apple trees. The pinkish-white blossoms that pop out in April signify the start of the year for apple growers. This is also the month for final equipment repair, and the start of irrigation that continues through the summer. Orchard grasses thrive with all that water, so growers mow orchards throughout the season to allow easy access to the trees.

Pollination begins in April and can continue into May. Natural pollination is impossible in most areas where apples are grown commercially. In Washington State alone, there are close to forty-eight hundred orchards simultaneously in bloom. To resolve this overabundance of flowers and lack of bees, apple growers rent colonies of bees from traveling beekeepers. Rented out in colonies of twenty-five thousand to forty thousand, honey bees can successfully pollinate the average thirty-five-acre orchard in one to four days.

By June, blossoms have transformed into small apples that are thinned by hand to assure the best balance between fruit size and quantity. Although most pruning occurs in winter, some is necessary in July to increase the amount of sunlight into trees. At this time, growers fertilize the orchards and place wooden props under tree limbs. Without the support, limbs would break under a tree's six-hundred- to seven-hundred-pound harvest.

Limb-propping and irrigation tasks continue through August. In mid-August, thousands of wooden picking bins are distributed throughout the orchards. In October, growers clean up the orchards, remove and stack props, and winterize irrigation systems. November's cold nights causes trees to go into dormancy. Pruning and equipment repair continue through March and the arrival of spring. Growers use a variety of strategies to warm the orchards and save the fruit buds from the

potentially damaging spring frosts. Early spring is also the time for planting new apple trees.

Apple growers spend a lot of time out of the orchard as well. They are responsible for all the accounting and management duties that come from running a business. Owners of large farm operations spend most of their time concentrating on business aspects, and hire farm workers to take care of the orchards. Besides knowing agriculture, apple growers need to understand biology, chemistry, economics, marketing, and computer science.

Rachel Carson

Scientists today study nature's interdependency—how each part depends on other parts in order to survive. Scientists also study the effects of human activity on nature and work on ways to prevent modern technology from harming animals, plants, and habitats. But not long ago, scientists didn't know that industrialization could permanently devastate habitats. When Rachel Carson, a biologist and writer, published her book *Silent Spring* in 1962, she shocked scientists and others into realizing that human activity could cause severe ecological damage.

In *Silent Spring,* Carson carefully detailed how random spraying of some pesticides caused terrible biological destruction. For example, she showed that the pesticide DDT didn't just kill insects. It also got into the bodies of small animals that ate the plants or drank from DDT-infested water. These animals were then eaten by larger animals. By this point the DDT was so concentrated in the animals' systems, it caused sickness and sometimes death. Carson explained the biological and ecological principles that made certain pesticides incredibly harmful. The effect of her book was powerful. Immediately, the government banned DDT. Soon, people in government, industry, and science were debating the idea that modern technology could destroy our habitat, and eventually us. One editor described Carson's book this way: "A few thousand words from her, and the world took a new direction."

Today, most pesticides are safer than they were in 1962. This is important to agriculture, including the apple industry, which must use pesticides to keep apples worm-free and trees healthy. Carson provided a new perspective about the earth she had studied most of her life. Her book sparked a better understanding of how we must interact with nature.

Boxing Apples

1. A box plot is another way to display some important aspects

   of the mass data from your size _____ _____ apples.
                                         (#)   (variety)

   Use your stem plot to list the values of the mass for your 36 apples in order from least to greatest in the column to the right.

2. The lower quartile, median, and upper quartile divide the mass of your apples into four groups of roughly the same size.

   a. Find your median mass.

      median = _____ grams

   b. Find your lower quartile mass.

      lower quartile = _____ grams

   c. Find your upper quartile mass.

      upper quartile = _____ grams

3. The interquartile range (IQR) is the difference between the upper and lower quartiles. Find the IQR.

   IQR = _____ Grams

4. Your lower extreme is the smallest value in your data, and your upper extreme is the largest value in your data.

   lower extreme = _____ grams

   upper extreme = _____ grams

Mass
1. _____
2. _____
3. _____
4. _____
5. _____
6. _____
7. _____
8. _____
9. _____
(lower quartile)
10. _____
11. _____
12. _____
13. _____
14. _____
15. _____
16. _____
17. _____
18. _____
(median)
19. _____
20. _____
21. _____
22. _____
23. _____
24. _____
25. _____
26. _____
27. _____
(upper quartile)
28. _____
29. _____
30. _____
31. _____
32. _____
33. _____
34. _____
35. _____
36. _____

5. Follow the directions below to make a box plot display that highlights the median, the lower and upper quartiles, and the extremes.

   a. Turn a sheet of graph paper sideways and draw a horizontal line near the top edge.

   b. Construct a number line with an interval of two grams that includes the range between your smallest mass and largest mass.

   c. Below the number line, mark points representing these five values:

   median _____

   lower quartile _____   lower extreme _____

   upper quartile _____   upper extreme _____

   d. Draw a box between the lower and upper quartiles as shown in the example below.

   e. Mark the median with a vertical line inside the box.

   f. Draw two lines (whiskers) from the quartiles to the extremes.

   An Example of a Box Plot

   lower   lower   median   upper   upper
   extreme   quartile   quartile   extreme

6. About what percent of your apple mass values are:

   Below the median? _____ Below the lower quartile? _____

   Above the lower quartile? _____ In the box? _____

   In each "whisker"? _____

7. Are the whiskers equal in length? If not, what does this mean?

8. Is the median in the center of the box? Why, or why not?

9. What are the advantages and disadvantages of using a box plot compared to a line or stem plot?

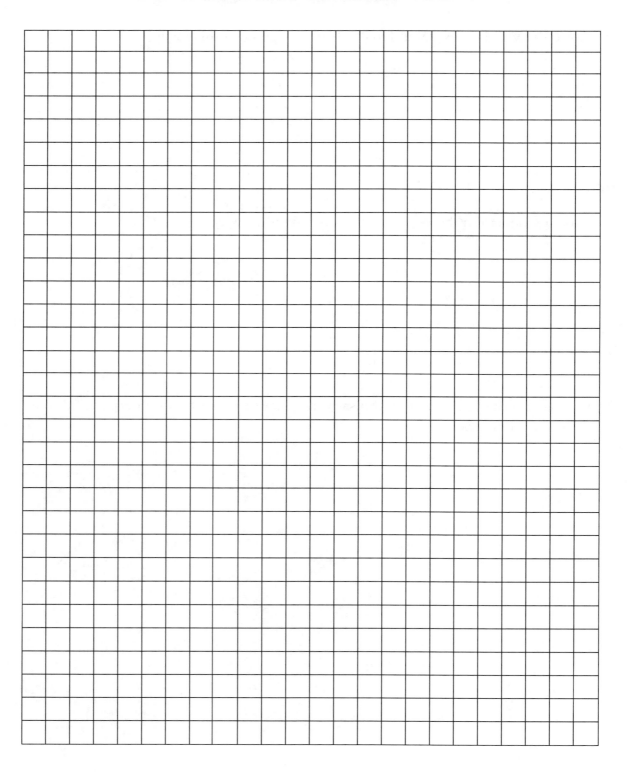

Branching Out

Box plots are useful for comparing data on the mass of several varieties of size

_____ apples.
    (#)

1. Calculate the information necessary to construct box plots representing the data from the other apple varieties measured in class.

_____ Apples   _____ Apples
    (variety)   (variety)

2. Construct box plots for these varieties directly below your existing apple box plot. Be sure to label each plot with the appropriate variety of apple.

3. Examine the three box plots. Are they the same? How do they vary?

4. Look at the box plots to decide which variety of apple has the largest interquartile range. Which variety is it?

5. On separate paper, write a paragraph giving an overall summary of the three box plots. Describe how the mass of your apples compare to the mass of other varieties in the class.

6. Who might be interested in this information? Why?

7. What kind of predictions can you make based on your interpretations?

8. What additional data might you collect in order to verify or disprove your conclusions?

Months (columns): JAN | FEB | MAR | APR | MAY | JUN | JUL | AUG | SEP | OCT | NOV | DEC

TREE DEVELOPMENT

- Dormant (JAN)
- Bud Development (MAR)
- Tree/Shoot Growth (JUN–JUL)
- Buds Formed (SEP)
- Hardening Off (NOV)
- Dormant (DEC)

FRUIT DEVELOPMENT

- Flower Set (APR)
- Bloom (MAY)
- Pollination (MAY)
- Fruit Set (MAY)
- Cell Division (MAY)
- Cell Enlargement (AUG)
- Color Development (OCT)
- Ripening (OCT)

FACTORS AFFECTING FRUIT SIZE, QUALITY, AND QUANTITY

- Pruning/Tree Vigor
- Soil Fertility (MAR–APR)
- Pollination (MAY)
- Cell Division (JUN)
- Thinning (Chemical and Hand) (JUN)
- Leaf Surface (Photosynthesis) (JUL)
- Insects and Disease (JUL)
- Shade Canopy (JUL)
- Cell Enlargement (Temperature Extremes) (AUG)
- Color Development (SEP)
- Sunburn (SEP)
- Harvest Management (OCT)

CULTURAL ACTIVITIES

- Pruning (JAN)
- Planting (MAR)
- Remove Brush (MAR)
- Fertilize (APR)
- Frost Control (APR)
- Chemical Thinning (MAY)
- Irrigation (Including Frost, Protection, and Overhead Cooling) (MAY)
- Insecticides (JUN)
- Herbicide (JUN)
- Hand Thinning (JUL)
- Mowing (6X) (JUL)
- Summer Prune (AUG)
- Fertilize (AUG)
- Herbicide (AUG)
- Propping (AUG)
- Harvest (SEP)
- Mowing (1X) (OCT)
- Herbicide (NOV)
- Orchard Cleanup (NOV)
- Pruning (DEC)
- Fertilize (Soil Application) (DEC)

ACTIVITY
4

APPLE STATISTICS

Overview

Students collect data on the heights and diameters of the three varieties of size-80 apples used in Activity 1. They prepare and examine line plots, stem plots, and box plots to further investigate questions that relate to the size of an apple. Box plots are used to compare the different varieties of apples. The role of statistics in improving and monitoring apple-storage procedures is presented.

Time. One or two 40- to 50-minute class periods.

Purpose. Students extend their experience with statistical displays. Through their observations and data analysis they assess the effectiveness of various plots in determining the mass, height, and diameter of a size-80 apple.

Materials. *For the teacher:*
◆ Transparency Master 4.5
◆ 1 size-80 apple
◆ Kitchen paring knife

For the student:
◆ Student Sheets 4.1–4.4
◆ Multiple copies of Student Sheet 4.2
◆ A pair of disposable latex gloves
◆ Centimeter ruler

For each group of students:
◆ 2–3 kitchen paring knives
◆ 1 dozen apples in plastic bag from Activity 1
◆ Masking tape and a cutting board

Getting Ready

1. Duplicate Students Sheets 4.1–4.4, including multiple copies of 4.2.
2. Prepare transparency of Student Sheet 3.2 with box plots of mass data for all three varieties.
3. Retrieve nine labeled bags of size-80 apples from the refrigerator.
4. Locate knives, masking tape, centimeter rulers, disposable latex gloves, and cutting boards.

Background Information

At this point, students have been introduced to statistics, line plots, stem plots, and box plots. They have prepared at least one of each type of plot, participated in discussions concerning the advantages and disadvantages of the displays, and, perhaps, drawn some conclusions about the sizing of apples based on their data.

This activity provides students additional experience with preparing displays and analyzing data as they collect information on the dimensions of size-80 apples. They display both the height data and the diameter data as line plots, stem plots, and box plots, and discuss the advantages and disadvantages of each type of plot. The History Link about Gertrude Mary Cox or the Technology Link "Controlled-Atmosphere Storage" can be used at any time during this activity to stimulate student interest. Students should work in the same groups as in Activity 1. Students collect data on the height and the diameter of each apple, as they explore the role that height, diameter, and mass have in determining an apple's official size.

Students need not collect data on apples in another size category to verify the effects of dimension and mass on determining the size of an apple. Apples of different sizes within the same variety are similar, therefore their dimensions and masses will be proportional. As the dimensions of an object change by a factor of x, the surface area is altered by x^2, and the volume or mass varies by x^3. According to Transparency Master 4.5, the dimension of a size-80 apple is ~80 mm, and it mass is ~238 grams. An apple scaled down by a factor of $\frac{3}{4}$ would be ~60 mm in dimension, a size 198. Its mass would be equivalent to $\left(\frac{3}{4}\right)^3 \cdot 238$ or $\frac{27}{64} \cdot 238$ grams, which is ~100 grams and corresponds to the estimated mass for a size 198 apple, ~108 grams.

Transparency Master 4.5 gives the apple size by mass and dimension. In talking with representatives from the apple industry, it is not clear what dimension is represented in this table. One task of this activity is to determine if dimension in Transparency Master 4.5 is best represented by height or by diameter. Recall, the size of the apple is determined by the number of apples that fit in a 42 pound box. Apple size is related to mass; 80 size-80 apples have a mass of 42 pounds.

Whereas the mass data for size-80 apples is spread out, a stem plot of the dimension data is so clustered that it becomes necessary to expand it by preparing one or more spread-out stem plots to determine the shape of the data.

In the examples below, "Spread-Out Stem Plot I" plots the leaves 0, 1, 2, 3, and 4 on the first line of the stem, and the leaves 5, 6, 7, 8, and 9 on the second line. "Spread-Out Stem Plot II" spreads out the data even further. Leaves 0 and 1 are on the first stem, 2 and 3 on the second, 4 and 5 on the third, and so on.

Stem Plots for Heights of Size-80 Rome Beauty Apples

Stem Plot

6|1 represents
61 millimeters

```
6 | 1 4 4 5 5 5 5 5 5 6 6 6 6 7 7 8 8 9 9 9
7 | 0 0 0 0 0 0 0 0 0 0 1 1 1 1
```

Spread-Out Stem Plot I

6|1 represents
61 millimeters

```
6 | 1 4 4
* | 5 5 5 5 5 6 6 6 6 7 7 8 8 9 9 9
7 | 0 0 0 0 0 0 0 0 0 0 1 1 1 1
```

Spread-Out Stem Plot II

6|1 represents
61 millimeters

```
6 | 1
* |
* | 4 4 5 5 5 5 5 5
* | 6 6 6 6 7 7
* | 8 8 9 9 9
7 | 0 0 0 0 0 0 0 0 0 0 1 1 1 1
```

The last plot seems to display the data best. The shape of the distribution is more apparent and gaps show up that are not visible in the other plots.

The back-to-back plot is yet another method used for comparing different sets of data. While it is not included on the student sheets, it could be used as an assessment activity.

Back-to-Back Spread-Out Stem Plot for Dimension of Rome Beauty Apples

	Diameter		Height
6l1 represents 61 millimeters		6	1
		*	
		*	4 4 5 5 5 5 5 5
		*	6 6 6 6 6 7 7
		*	8 8 9 9 9
		7	0 0 0 0 0 0 0 0 0 0 0 0 1 1 1 1
		*	
		*	
	7 7 6	*	
	9 8 8 8	*	
	1 1 1 1 0 0 0 0 0 0 0 0 0 0 0 0	8	
	3 3 3 3 3 2 2 2	*	
	5 5 4	*	
	7 6	*	
		*	
		9	
	1	*	

The mass, height, and diameter results for each variety of apples and the variability between the different varieties may suggest a basis for the characteristics that determine a size-80 apple. Then again, this activity may only compound the issue by creating more questions, and serve to give a realistic sense of what can and does happen in a statistical study.

Presenting The Activity

Show Transparency Master 4.5. The table states that the mass for a size-80 apple is 238 grams. Ask:

◆ Is the mass of all size-80 apples exactly 238 grams?

◆ What aspects, if any, of your data does this relate to?

◆ How do you think they arrived at the information in the table?

The table claims that a size-80 apple is 80 millimeters in "dimension." Ask:

◆ What dimension could this be?

◆ How can you find out?

Tell students that in this activity they will explore answers to this question by collecting, organizing, and evaluating height and diameter data on the same apples used in Activity 1.

Measuring Apples. Divide students into the three groups from Activity 1. Hand out Student Sheets 4.1–4.2 along with the apples and the necessary materials for completing the activity. Have them decide who in their group will measure the heights and who will measure the diameters. Have them respond to question 4 on Student Sheet 4.1.

Demonstrate the appropriate way to use a kitchen paring knife to accurately cut an apple in half vertically. Discuss how to measure an apple's height and diameter. Since an apple is not necessarily symmetric, suggest that they measure the highest portion and widest place on each apple half. Tell students to make sure each half of the apple has the same number on it (written on a piece of masking tape). Have them begin to collect and record their data while you interact with the groups to make sure they are proceeding safely.

Packaging the Apples for Family Activity. As the groups finish measuring the heights and diameters of their apples, have them package the apples for the Family Activity. There should be 36 packages of 3 apple halves each, one half of each variety. Have the students, using masking tape, label the apples with their varieties. You will need to organize the movement of bags from one group to another to ensure that each bag has one apple of each of the three varieties.

Plotting the Data. Not all groups will complete the data collection at the same time. Having students make line plots of data from their 12 apples will give time for all groups to complete the data collection. Help students exchange the additional data they need to expand their line plots. They should continue working in their groups to complete Student Sheets 4.1 and 4.3.

Hand out both pages of Student Sheet 4.4, and referring to the background information about spread-out stem plots, discuss question 3. Some students may benefit from making yet a third stem plot of their dimension data that will spread out the distribution further.

As they analyze their box plots, remind the class that even though box plots seem to be the most difficult plot to construct, they are the best method to use for a direct comparison of the medians, extremes, and quartiles of several data sets. With their assistance, list the possible comparisons to be considered on the board or overhead. Include height to diameter for a specific variety, the heights or diameters for all three varieties, and the heights to the diameters for all three varieties.

Suggest that three students display their box plots for the heights of the three varieties of size-80 apples on a transparency of Student Sheet 4.2.

Designate three other students to display their box plots depicting the diameter measurements on another transparency of Student Sheet 4.2 in the same order and position using a different color overhead pen. Now place the two transparencies on top of each other with the grids coinciding. Use the results to conduct a discussion and analysis of the data.

Have students look again at the data on Transparency Master 4.5. Ask:

◆ What do you think "dimension" means?

◆ Does the class data agree with the premise that a size-80 apple has dimension 80? And if so, what dimension is it?

◆ How do you think size is determined?

Discussion Questions

1. How does the range of the height data compare to the range of the mass data?

2. How does the range of the diameter data compare to the range of the mass data?

3. How does the range of the diameter data compare to the range of the height data?

4. Discuss your opinion of each type of statistical display, and how each one conveys a different perspective.

Assessment Questions

1. Work with someone in another group to prepare a back-to-back spread-out stem plot for the heights or diameters for two varieties of apples. Describe the information conveyed by this plot.

2. Prepare box plots for the mass data, the height data, and the diameter data for your variety of size-80 apples. Analyze and describe the display.

3. Work with students from two other groups to prepare a box plot for the masses, heights, or diameters of all 9 dozen size-80 apples. Analyze and describe the distribution.

Gertrude Mary Cox

Gertrude Mary Cox began her career as a statistician at Iowa State University. She helped her professor create better statistical methods to deal with the practical problems of agricultural research. That was in the late 1920s. By 1931, she received the first master's degree in statistics given by Iowa State's department of statistics. She became so busy teaching and consulting for the university, she couldn't find time to write a doctoral dissertation. Nevertheless, the dean was so impressed with her work, he awarded her an honorary Doctor of Science at the school's centennial celebration, saying, "Her influence (in statistics) is worldwide."

In 1945, Cox organized and became director of the Institute of Statistics, in North Carolina. She established workshops on statistics in plant science, agricultural economics, taste testing, and other subjects. Under her direction, the Institute of Statistics became an international center for statistics.

Cox's main goal was to spread statistical learning programs throughout the Southern states. Her objective became known as "spreading the gospel according to St. Gertrude." It worked. The Southern Regional Education Board agreed to establish a committee on statistics to help improve statistical understanding and provide statistical consulting in the South.

In her lifetime Cox published over 16 articles and books on statistics. Even in retirement she strived to increase statistical competency in the world—she helped develop statistical programs in Egypt and Thailand, and was consultant to government agencies and other groups. Gertrude Cox died of leukemia at 78 on October 17, 1978.

Controlled-Atmosphere Storage

The single most important scientific contribution to the apple industry has been the technological development and refinement of Controlled Atmosphere storage (CA). CA was developed shortly after World War II. It involves harvesting the best apples at just the right time and placing them in large airtight refrigerated rooms where the temperature, oxygen, carbon dioxide, and humidity are carefully controlled and regulated. This halts the apple's natural ripening process.

Harvested fruit breathes. It uses up oxygen and carbohydrates and gives off carbon dioxide, water, and heat. The faster the respiration (breathing), the faster the fruit ripens. Refrigeration slows down the apple's respiration. So does lowering the oxygen level of the atmosphere, setting the temperature at 30–31 degrees Fahrenheit, and increasing carbon dioxide to specified levels. This process of Controlled Atmosphere extends the apple's shelf life and makes it possible for apples harvested in the fall to be available all year. CA also reduces the need for apple growers to plant a succession of apple varieties maturing from early summer to late winter.

The apples you find most of in the stores are probably those that survive best in CA storage. You would not be able to tell the difference between an apple picked one week ago and an apple picked five months ago because both would have crisp, tasty flesh and smooth skin. Scientists have done extensive testing and statistical analysis to find the precise combination of temperature and carbon dioxide, the optimum time for harvesting, the varieties of apples that are best suited for CA, and length of time in storage so that the stored apples will taste just as good as the fresh ones.

Measuring Apples

1. My group is collecting data on the heights and diameters of size _____
   (#)
   _____ apples.
   (variety of apple)

2. My group is measuring the same apples that we found the masses of, apples numbered:

   A. 1–12   B. 13–24   C. 25–36

3. Collect the data by following the directions below:
   a. Some people should measure the height of each apple, and others should measure the diameter. Decide who will measure what.
   b. Use a knife to carefully cut each apple in half vertically. Be sure to label both halves with the same number.
   c. Measure the height and the diameter of each of your 12 apples to the nearest millimeter and record the result in the table on the following page.

4. Should you measure both halves of the same apple? Explain.

5. Using masking tape, label each apple as to variety. Following directions from your teacher, package the apples in plastic bags. The packaging should result in 36 bags, each bag containing three half apples, one half of each variety.

_____ Apples
(apple variety)

Number	H	D	Number	H	D	Number	H	D
1			13			25		
2			14			26		
3			15			27		
4			16			28		
5			17			29		
6			18			30		
7			19			31		
8			20			32		
9			21			33		
10			22			34		
11			23			35		
12			24			36		

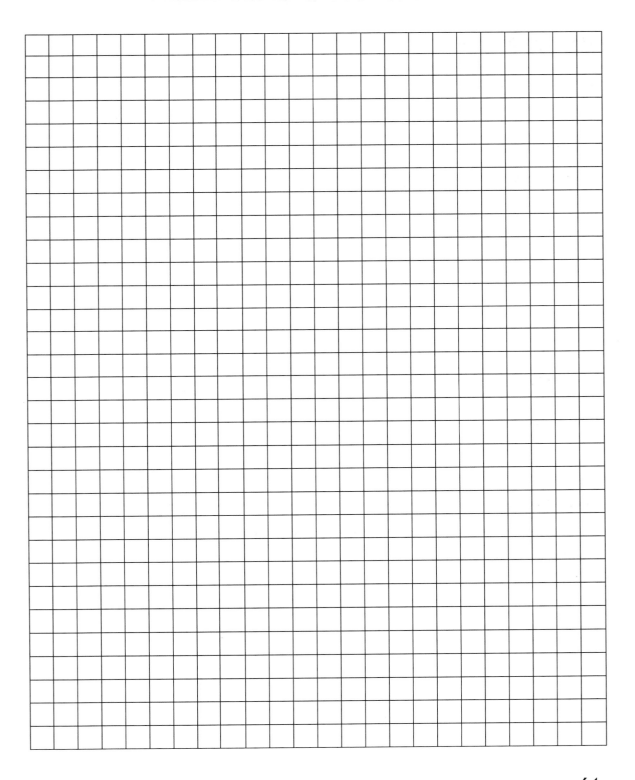

Displaying Apples

Line Plot for 12 Apples

1. The range of the _____ for these 12 apples is between

   _____ and _____ mm.

2. Prepare a line plot of your data with a one millimeter interval.

3. Describe the distribution of your data, including discussion of clusters, gaps, outliers, and location of the median.

4. Do you feel confident about your observations based on the size of your sample? Explain.

Line Plot for 36 Apples

5. Complete the table on Student Sheet 4.1 by collecting the remaining data from your classmates.

6. Add the new data for _____ to your line plot.

7. Describe the distribution of the larger sample.

8. Did enlarging the sample size affect the distribution? Explain.

Different Displays

Your group is going to display the height and diameter data for all 36 apples in two more modes—stem-and-leaf plots and box plots. Some members of the group should make the plots for the height, and others should make the plots for the diameter. Decide who will make which plots.

Stem Plot

1. Prepare a stem plot of your data.

2. What conclusions can you make by looking at the stem plot you just constructed?

3. If there are too many leaves per stem, spread out the stem plot as shown and reorganize it.

```
6 | 2 2 4        Put the leaves for 0, 1, 2, 3, and 4 on the first line for each
* | 5 6          stem and the leaves 5, 6, 7, 8, and 9 on the second line.
7 |
* |
```

4. Which of the two stem plots do you think displays the data best? Why?

Box Plot Display

5. Use either of your stem plots to locate the five important values necessary for making a box plot.

   median _____

   lower quartile _____   lower extreme _____

   upper quartile _____   upper extreme _____

6. Determine the interquartile range.

7. Prepare a box plot representing your data with an interval of one millimeter.

8. What does the location of the median tell you about the data?

Summary

9. On a separate sheet of paper, write a paragraph describing what you have learned from studying all three types of plots. Discuss the advantages and disadvantages of each type of display.

10. With your group, using the six displays for height and diameter, discuss how you would compare the height to the diameter for your apple variety. Write a brief summary of the process.

11. With your group, use the three displays for height or the three for diameter to discuss how you would compare the heights or diameters of your apples to the other varieties. Be prepared to describe your process to the class.

12. Your data is for size _____ apples. How do you think the size of an apple is determined?   (#)

Apple Size

Size	Mass in Grams	Dimension in mm
48	397	91
56	340	88
64	298	85
72	264	82
80	**238**	**80**
88	215	76
100	190	73
113	167	71
125	153	69
138	136	67
150	127	66
163	116	64
175	108	62
198	96	60
216	88	58

What dimension do you think the apple industry is using?

ACTIVITY
5

NEW
RELATIONS

Overview

Students investigate the relation between height and mass and the relation between diameter and mass by constructing and analyzing scatter plots. They analyze their scatter plots and relate their findings to the process of sizing apples. In conclusion, the students investigate the connection between height and diameter.

Time. One or two 40- to 50-minute class periods.

Purpose. Students are introduced to a new way of displaying data that has a very different basis from what they have been studying. A scatter plot is used for investigating relations between two characteristics. Relations between two characteristics or variables are called associations or correlations.

Materials. *For the teacher:*

◆ A transparency of Student Sheet 5.2

For the student:

◆ Student Sheets 5.1–5.3

◆ Multiple copies of Student Sheet 5.2

◆ A straightedge

Getting Ready

1. Duplicate Students Sheets 5.1–5.3, including multiple copies of 5.2.
2. Prepare a transparency of Student Sheet 5.2

Background Information

Students have investigated different ways to organize and display information on one characteristic or variable. They have constructed and analyzed line plots, stem plots, and box plots for the distribution of apple mass, apple height, and apple diameter. These plots display the distribution of each of these dimensions independently. In this activity, students investigate the relation between two of these variables. They construct scatter plots in which one variable is plotted on the horizontal axis and the second variable is plotted on the vertical axis.

Scatter plots display the relation or association between two variables. The association can be grouped into three broad categories:

◆ If an increase in one variable, say the diameter, is related to an increase in the second variable, say mass, it is called a positive association.

◆ If an increase in one variable is related to a decrease in the second variable, it is called a negative association.

◆ If neither appears to be the case, if the points appear to be scattered at random, one says there is no association.

The example below illustrates a positive association in which the points are scattered around a line that appears to be going from the lower left corner of the plot to the upper right corner of the plot. As one variable increases, so does the other, that is, both are increasing.

Scatter plot showing positive association

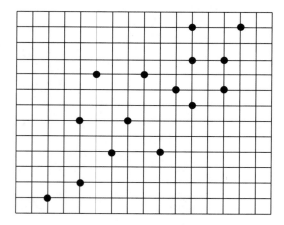

Note in the following example, showing a negative association, that the points are scattered around a line that appears to be running from the upper left of the plot to the lower right. As one variable increases, the other decreases, that is, there is an inverse relationship between the two variables.

Scatter plot showing negative association

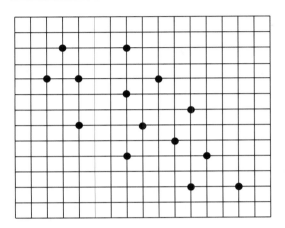

In the example below, illustrating no association, the points appear to be scattered all over the place. Sometimes it is difficult to distinguish between weak associations and no association. A general rule is that if you can cover one or two points and make it appear that there is no association, then probably there isn't.

Scatter plot showing no association

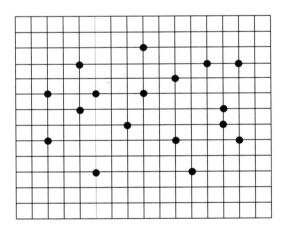

Students are aware of the wide use of associations, more frequently called correlations. Positive associations are commonly called positive correlations, negative associations are called negative correlations, and the case of no association is described as no correlation. One of the most commonly reported association is that between smoking and lung cancer.

A discussion of the correlation between cigarette smoking and lung cancer can lead to a discussion of a common misinterpretation of correlation. A positive correlation is frequently interpreted as a cause and effect relation. This is not necessarily the case. In the case of cigarette smoking and lung cancer, a positive correlation was observed, which led the medical profession to further investigation. The results of the medical research indicated a cause-effect relation between cigarette smoking and lung cancer.

Shoe size and mathematics scores are positively associated. As shoe size increases, mathematics scores increase. However, there is no cause-effect relation. Both shoe size and mathematics scores are correlated to growth, and growth causes an increase in shoe size and, indirectly, in mathematics scores.

Correlations are one of the critical first steps in research. Observations frequently lead to hypotheses, and one of the first steps is to verify the assumed relation. If correlations are found, either positive or negative, further research follows in an attempt to ascertain additional variables involved, or to find cause and effect relations.

Presenting the Activity

The students were introduced to the idea of comparing height to diameter in question 10 on Student Sheet 4.4. You might start the discussion with groups describing the process they proposed for investigating this question. Orchestrate the discussion toward hypotheses on the association between height and diameter, including the rationale for any hypothesis.

Elicit from the class a definition, description, or example of an association or correlation. Point out that the words are used interchangeably. Orchestrate the discussion to ensure that the class fully understands the concept of association between two variables.

Hand out Student Sheets 5.1–5.2. Group the students according to the variety of apples on which they have been working. The groups are to make two scatter plots, one illustrating the relation between diameter and mass, and one illustrating the relation between height and mass. Have the students in each group decide who will work on each plot. Work with each group to ensure that the scatter-plot grids are correctly set up and labeled and that the students are accurately plotting the coordinates. If you observe that many students are encountering difficulty with the process, use a transparency of Student Sheet 5.2 and work with the class in plotting a few points.

When all groups have completed Student Sheet 5.1 and have had a few minutes to read and discuss question 1 on Student Sheet 5.3, orchestrate a class discussion on the different types of associations. You might want to make a transparency of the scatter plots on pages 68 and 69 to use in the discussion, or you could elicit from the class what they think a scatter plot illustrating a positive relation would look like and draw it, or have a student draw it, on a transparency of Student Sheet 5.2.

Question 1 on Student Sheet 5.3 needs to be started in class, however, it could be completed as homework, as could the remainder of the sheet.

The Career Link "Food Scientists" and the Technology Link "Apple in a Can" provide interesting background reading about food science.

Discussion Questions

1. Is there an association between height and mass? Between diameter and mass?

2. Are height and diameter correlated? If so, is it a cause-effect relation?

3. Describe an association that you have heard about that you suspect is a cause-effect relation.

4. Describe an association that you have heard about that you suspect is not a cause-effect relation.

Assessment Questions

1. Describe an investigation in which a scatter plot would be more appropriate than a stem or box plot. Explain your thinking.

2. Prepare a scatter plot for height versus diameter for all three varieties of size-80 apples measured in the class. Analyze and describe the display.

3. Scan the newspapers or magazines in your home or school library for reports utilizing scatter plots. After reading the report, analyze the plot and critique the report.

Food Scientists

The people responsible for creating and testing the blends of apple juice are food scientists. Food scientists use the laws of science and engineering to produce, process, evaluate, package, and distribute foods. They may concentrate on basic research, product development, quality control, processing, packaging, technical sales, or market research.

Many food scientists study the properties of food, why food deteriorates or spoils, and how companies can improve processing of foods for the public. They often work for a large processing company that has a test kitchen where they experiment with different formulas until they get the best product possible. In developing new products and processes, they may also work with microbiologists, flavor experts, packaging specialists, and statisticians.

The food processing industry is vital to the economy. About 40,000 food scientists work throughout the United States with close to 75 percent of them involved in the food-processing industry. If you want to become a food scientist, be sure to take English, biology, chemistry, physics, and mathematics in high school. You should work on expressing your ideas well, both verbally and in writing, since communication is an essential part of the profession. An inquiring mind and a problem-solving attitude will also help you.

Because of the growing need to improve the quantity, quality, variety, and safety of foods, there aren't enough graduates to fill the available job positions. The demand for food scientists will continue to increase around the world.

Apple in a Can

For thousands of years people salted, dried, smoked, pickled, and chilled their foods. But today, food can be frozen, canned, or even freeze-dried. These are recent technologies, and they are still being improved. Scientific researchers continue to find new and better ways to process, package, and preserve foods. Take, for example, apples.

Not all apples make it to the fresh-produce department of the store. About 55 percent does, but the other 45 percent is processed into applesauce, apple juice and cider, frozen apples, apple butter, and other apple products. An estimated 1.7 billion gallons of apple juice are consumed in this country every year. That is approximately 50 billion bushels of apples.

Modern equipment and technologies have helped companies make better apple cider and juice, but the basic process of making cider hasn't changed much since the early 1600s. Apples are ground into "pomace," a pulpy substance, then pressed to get the juice. In pioneer times, farmers used a cider press of two flat boards fastened to a large screw and turned by hand. Now, heavy machinery does the job of squishing the juice out. Machines also strain the fresh juice to remove large particles. Little particles of apple left behind give the cider a cloudy look. The cider is allowed to mix with oxygen in the air to gets its dark amber color and distinctive flavor.

Apple juice is simply cider that is clarified through modern technology. "Clarified" means the tiny apple solids are removed to leave the juice clear and light colored. The juice is pasteurized and vacuum packed to keep it fresh for over a year without refrigeration. These techniques for storing pasteurized apple juice were perfected by the canning industry in the early 1940s.

Frozen concentrated apple juice is prepared by commercial processes. By removing the water, clarified juice becomes concentrated. It is then packed and frozen for storage. You can add water any time to return the juice to its original strength.

Scatter Plots

1. Do you think that there is a relation between the height or diameter of an apple and its mass? Explain.

2. A scatter plot can be used to further investigate this question. Complete the table for the variety of apples you measured.

_____ _____ **Apples**
(#)   (variety)

Number	H	D	Mass	Number	H	D	Mass	Number	H	D	Mass
1				13				25			
2				14				26			
3				15				27			
4				16				28			
5				17				29			
6				18				30			
7				19				31			
8				20				32			
9				21				33			
10				22				34			
11				23				35			
12				24				36			

3. Your group is going to make two different scatter plots; height versus mass, and diameter versus mass. Decide who in your group will work on which plot.

4. For each scatter plot, set up the grid on Student Sheet 5.2 with the height or diameter on the horizontal axis and the mass on the vertical axis. Label each axis, including the units. Construct each scatter plot by graphing the (H,M) or the (D,M) coordinate pair for each apple.

5. Describe the scatter plot you made.

6. Do you think there is a relation between the two variables in the scatter plot? Explain.

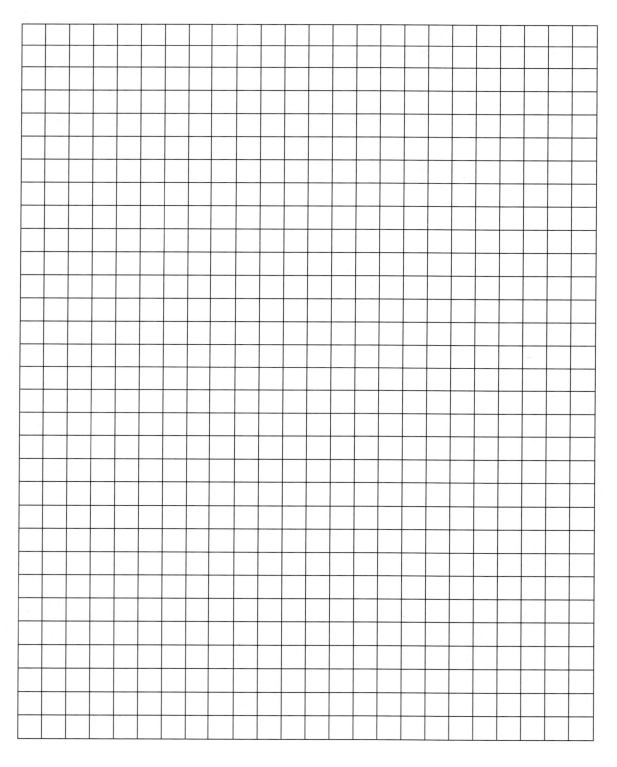

New Relations or No Relations

1. As a group, you are to compare the two scatter plots. After ample discussion, write a brief description (on a separate sheet of paper) of the information conveyed by the scatter plots. Include discussion of the following topics:

   a. If an increase in one variable (height) is related to an increase in the other variable (mass), this is called a positive relation or a positive association. If an increase in one variable is related to a decrease in the other variable, this is called a negative association. If neither appears to be the case, one says there is no association.

      ◆ How would you describe the association between height and mass?
      ◆ Between diameter and mass?
      ◆ Are the associations the same?
      ◆ Which dimension, height or diameter, is more closely associated with mass?

   b. Clusters of points, gaps, and outliers can exist in a scatter plot just as they can exist in line or stem plots.

      ◆ What does a cluster tell you?
      ◆ What do gaps tell you?
      ◆ Any outliers? What do they tell you?

2. Construct a scatter plot for height versus diameter, and write a brief summary of your findings, including discussion of the above points.

FAMILY
ACTIVITY

STATISTICAL
SLICES

Overview

Students are given an apple taste-test package containing three varieties of apples. They conduct a survey and opinion poll with their families on the flavor and texture of each variety, rating the taste of each on a scale of 1–5. The collective data from the families will be organized, displayed, and analyzed in class.

Time. At least one hour at home, plus one or two 40- to 50-minute class periods (this activity can be done anytime following Activity 4).

Purpose. Students and their families participate in an apple taste-test survey. The extensive data is organized and partially analyzed in class, with the analysis being completed at home by the family groups.

Materials. *For the teacher:*

◆ Transparency of Family Activity Sheet 5

For each student:

◆ Family Activity Sheets 1–6

◆ 3–4 copies of Family Activity Sheet 2, depending on family size

◆ Family taste-test package prepared in Activity 4

For each group of students:

◆ Completed survey slips from one variety of apple

Getting Ready

1. Duplicate Family Activity Sheets 1–6, including multiple copies of Family Activity Sheet 2.

2. Retrieve family taste-test packages from the refrigerator.

Background Information

Our society is constantly influenced by statistical surveys as each member makes consumer choices and economic and political decisions. Surveys are carried out by governments, universities, businesses, companies, political candidates, and non-profit groups. The results of these surveys appear in magazines and newspapers and are discussed on television and radio.

A common type of survey is the opinion poll. A statistician, usually with a sociology or psychology background, conducts an opinion poll to discover what most people think about a product or issue by surveying a small portion of the population, called a sample. Samples are specifically chosen to represent a target group of individuals. For example, the target population for testing apple juice products could be mothers of children aged two to six. A small random percentage of the target population is chosen as a representative sample for a limited opinion poll.

National polls generally use samples of about 1,500 persons to reflect national attitudes and opinions. A sample of this size produces accurate estimates for a country as large as the United States with a population of over 200 million. Because a properly selected sample of only 1,500 individuals can reflect various characteristics of the total population within a very small margin of error, the value of surveys and their widespread use is clearly understandable. They provide a speedy and economical means of determining facts about our economy and people's knowledge, beliefs, expectations, and behavior.

Statisticians decide where to get the data, determine the type and size of the sample group, develop the survey questionnaire, and coordinate tabulating the returns. The Writing Link in this activity has students practice these tasks by making their own survey on other varieties of apples.

Improper sampling methods, especially voluntary response samples, occur often, especially through the news media and radio and television talk shows. This data provides no useful information about anyone except the people who chose to step forward. These unreliable and misleading forms of data collection make clear the need for random sampling—a scientific method for selecting samples.

This activity provides an opportunity for students to conduct a taste-test survey and analyze the results as another aspect of statistics. Collecting family data for the survey is relevant primarily to students in the class and their families and may or may not reflect the opinions of the whole school or their families.

Compiling, organizing, and interpreting the data from the taste test is the focus of Family Activity Sheets 3–6. Students are asked to select a plot that will best answer their questions about the data. Because of the limited whole number range of the rating scale, a stem plot is not particularly useful for displaying and interpreting the results. Students who choose this presentation should be encouraged to prepare the display and discuss the results with their group. They may discover for themselves the reasons for its ineffectiveness. A line plot gives an accurate assessment of the clusters and gaps, and an overall picture of the shape of the distribution. Another possible result of a taste-test survey could be that the median rating for each of the apples is the same, even though one person may prefer a variety that another person loathes, and vice versa. The sense of balance this creates is best evidenced in a box plot display.

Presenting the Activity

Ask students to share their knowledge of polls and surveys. Topics commonly mentioned are TV ratings, predictions for presidential elections, and marketing surveys conducted in shopping malls. Ask the students:

◆ Why would someone want to conduct a survey?

◆ What kind of questions do you think they ask?

◆ What kind of information is obtained from a poll or survey?

◆ How do you think the information is used?

◆ Do you think that surveys are reliable? Why, or why not?

Much reliance is placed upon surveys because of the quick and accurate information they provide on people's preferences, needs, and behavior. A corporation makes a survey of the potential market before introducing a new product. They may ask the public questions about the product and to rate it on some kind of scale.

Tell students that in a reputable survey, the sample population is not selected haphazardly or only from people who volunteer to participate. It is scientifically chosen so that each individual in the population is equally likely to be chosen, and the members of the sample are chosen independently of one another. This is called random sampling. Random samples can be difficult to obtain. If a sample tends to overrepresent or underrepresent some part of the population then the results are biased. Refer to the background information for more discussion about surveys and polls, or to *Exploring Surveys and Information from Samples* (see page xv).

Ask the following questions:

◆ Do your families represent a random sample of the local population? of the state population? Why, or why not?

◆ You and your families are going to participate in a apple taste-testing survey. Is there anything that might bias or influence you from making independent decisions as you describe the texture and rate the taste of each variety of apple?

◆ How could you minimize any possible biased opinions?

◆ What will the results of the taste test tell us?

Hand out Family Activity Sheets 1–3. Discuss with students how they might set up the family taste-test survey. Ask the students:

◆ What information should you give your family preceding the taste test?

◆ Should you tell them which varieties they are tasting before or after they've completed the test?

◆ Would knowing the name of each variety bias their decisions?

◆ Should you blindfold each person so that he or she can't see the apples?

◆ Does every person being tested need to be present at the same time?

◆ Should the tasters immediately complete the survey slip on an apple after tasting it, or taste them all and then complete the forms?

◆ Should they be allowed to taste more than one slice of a certain apple before recording their opinions?

◆ Does it matter how thick the slices are?

◆ Should you take part in the survey?

◆ Would student opinions be collected in the same manner, or analyzed separately?

You may use a transparency of Family Activity Sheet 2 to introduce and explain the rating scale for the survey. Convey that students are not necessarily comparing the apples. For example, a student may rank all of them a 5. Each variety should be judged on its own merit. Ask them to identify words that describe flavor, such as sweet, sour, salty, and spicy and words that describe the texture, such as smooth, crisp, or mushy.

As a class, the students need to agree on the final format and survey setup. It is important to collect all the family data in a similar manner in order to produce a valid sample for the class to analyze.

Distribute the apple taste-test packages, and make sure that students are able to accurately identify each variety of apple in their package.

As you discuss Family Activity Sheet 3, explain that each group will systematically tabulate the survey results for the variety of apple with which they have been working when they return to school the next day. Before distributing Family Activity Sheets 4–6 on the following day, conduct an informal discussion on their reactions to the taste test. Ask if there were any surprises.

Distribute Family Activity Sheets 4–5 and ask students to work as a group in organizing the results of the survey. Explain that they will start the analysis in class, and complete it at home with their family. Give each group the appropriate survey forms. Suggest that they work in teams of four and divide the forms among these teams to partially tabulate the results. Two of the members could record the ratings while two list the flavor descriptions. A person from each taste and flavor team could work with their counterparts to conclude the data distribution, and then return to their team of four to complete questions 4–7.

As you hand out Family Activity Sheet 6, remind students that they need to complete Family Activity Sheet 5 (collect all the survey data) in order to complete the analysis at home. You may prepare a transparency of Family Activity Sheet 5 to facilitate the recording of the family data.

When the students and their families have completed Family Activity Sheet 6, orchestrate a discussion focused on their findings. Since each group might have focused on a different piece of information from the survey, allow time for each group to present their findings and those of the families. Include a discussion of the family responses to the texture and flavor as well as taste. Look for common as well as opposing descriptions.

If you decide to have students do the Writing Link focused on developing their own surveys, first discuss the information about surveys provided in the background information.

Though the suggested time for this family activity recommends at least one hour, the actual time required will vary from student to student. Give them a reasonable length of time, perhaps two to four days spanning a weekend, to complete the study. They may need this extension to arrange adequate time with each family member to conduct the taste tests.

Discussion Questions

1. Discuss the idea of sample size. What would the results look like if just the students had done the taste test? What size sample is needed to have reliable results?

2. How do the flavors, textures, or tastes compare among the varieties?

3. Do you think that the results obtained from the taste-test survey might be biased? Give reasons. How might you minimize bias?

4. What did you like best about doing the survey?

Taste Test

With your family or friends, conduct your own taste test using more varieties of apples than those provided in the Family Activity. Grocery stores in your area will probably carry the three varieties used in the Family Activity, plus other selections that you may have never tasted before. Try to find samples of some unusual varieties, such as Fuji. Try to find five or more varieties to use in the survey. Create your own survey slips or copy the ones on Family Activity Sheet 2. Have the tasters describe the flavor on the slip and rate the taste. After having as many tasters as you can (including yourself) sample the apples, statistically analyze the data by creating a plot display. Choose the display you think will work best (line plot, bar plot, scatter plot, or stem plot). Write a short paragraph describing your findings. What conclusions can you make?

Family Taste Test

Materials You Will Need

◆ The Family Activity taste-test package of apples

◆ A kitchen paring knife

◆ 3 plates, one for each variety of apple

◆ Survey slips, 3 for each family member—1 for each variety of apple

◆ Scissors

◆ Pencil or pen

◆ Family Activity Sheet 3

Getting Ready

Follow the directions given below for each variety of apples separately. Remove the variety label from each apple half. Put one label on or near the plate on which you will place the slices of this variety. Wash the apples with soap and water. Rinse well in cold water. Using a paring knife, take a slice off the exposed part of the apple and discard it. Slice the apple halves into a sufficient number of pieces to allow each family member to have a piece to taste. Place all the slices on a plate.

After washing the paring knife, repeat this process for the other two varieties.

Cut Family Activity Sheets 2 into individual survey slips. You need 3 survey slips for each family member.

Conducting the Taste Test

1. Describe in detail the process that you will use to conduct your family taste-test survey. Use a separate sheet of paper.

2. Discuss the project with each person you are surveying and conduct the apple taste test.

3. When everyone has completed the taste test on all three varieties of apples, complete Family Activity Sheet 3.

Survey Slips

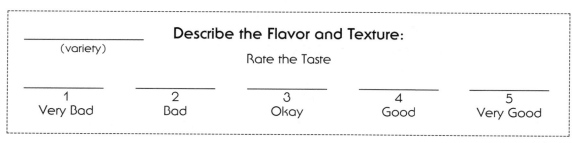

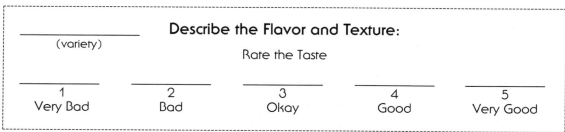

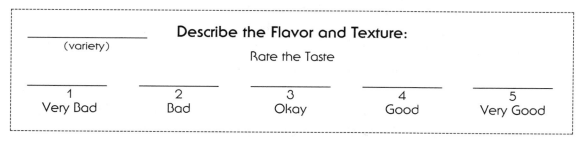

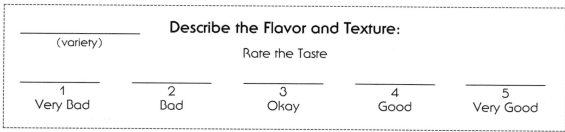

Describe the Flavor and Texture:

_____
(variety)

Rate the Taste

| 1 | 2 | 3 | 4 | 5 |
| Very Bad | Bad | Okay | Good | Very Good |

Family Responses

1. Use the table below to organize your family data. List the ratings for each family member for each variety. It will facilitate the work in class if you group the responses by variety rather than family member. For example, list all the responses to one type of apple before you list any responses to the next type.

Family Taste-Test Ratings

Variety	Name	Taste Rating	Texture Description

2. Did anything surprise you about your results? If so, explain.

3. With your family, write a brief summary of your taste-test results.

4. Take this sheet and all the completed survey slips to class tomorrow.

Survey Analysis

1. My group is organizing the taste-test data for _____ apples.
    (variety)

2. Which variety of apples do you think will receive the best ratings from the family survey? Why?

3. As a group, record the information from all surveys slips for _____ apples onto Family Activity Sheet 5.
    (variety)

4. What would you like to learn from the taste-test survey data that has been collected?

5. Select a plot that will give you information to answer your question. Construct it on graph paper.

6. Write a brief summary of the details in the plot, and your conclusions.

7. Discuss your plot and interpretations with other members in your group. Do they agree with your conclusions? Explain.

Apple Taste-Test Ratings

Family Name	_____ (variety)	_____ (variety)	_____ (variety)
1.			
2.			
3.			
4.			
5.			
6.			
7.			
8.			
9.			
10.			
11.			
12.			
13.			
14.			
15.			
16.			
17.			
18.			
19.			
20.			
21.			
22.			
23.			
24.			
25.			
26.			
27.			
28.			
29.			
30.			

Survey Analysis II

1. Complete Family Activity Sheet 5 by obtaining the survey data for the other varieties of apples from the other groups.

2. Take the plot you constructed for Family Activity Sheet 4 and 2 pieces of graph paper home. Discuss it with your family, and working with them, construct the same type of plot for the other varieties.

3. Compare the results for all three apple varieties. Any surprises? Explain.

4. From your analysis, what can you conclude about the taste preference for these apples?

COMPLETED
STUDENT
SHEETS

10. Put your apples in a plastic bag. Label it and give it to your teacher.

11. A line plot is a quick way to organize and visualize your data. Use Student Sheet 1.2 and follow these steps to prepare a line plot representing the mass of apples in your sample.

Turn your graph paper sideways and draw a horizontal line near the bottom edge.

Put a number scale on this line. Since the smallest apple in your sample is _____ grams, and the largest is _____ grams, your scale should include these numbers.

Plot your apple data by marking an "x" above the line at the appropriate mass.

If more than one apple has the same mass, put the additional points one unit above the other, stacking them on the graph.

12. Describe what you observe about the masses of apples from your line plot.

Answers will vary, but should include reference to the differences in size even though they are all called the same size.

Apple Masses

1. My group is one of three groups collecting data on size _____ *Answers will vary.*
   (#) (variety of apple)
   apples.

2. There are _36_ apples in the three groups, and _12_ apples in my group's
   (#)   (#)
   sample.

3. The apples are to be numbered. Among the three groups decide which numbers each group will use. The apples in my group's sample will be numbered:

   A. 1–12   B. 13–24   C. 25–36

4. Use masking tape and label each apple in your sample with an appropriate number.

5. List the numbers of your apples in the left-hand column of the table.

6. If any of your apples have stems, remove them.

7. Use the balance to measure the mass of each apple in your sample to the nearest gram. Record the results in the table.

8. According to your sample, a _____ apple's mass is between _____ and _____ grams.

9. Line up your 12 apples in order from smallest to largest. What do you see?

Apple Data	
Number	Mass

Seeds for Thought

1. Enlarge your sample size by collecting data from the other two groups in your class measuring the same variety of apple. Record the information in the table below.

Mass of _Answers will vary_ **Apples**
(apple variety)

Number	Mass	Number	Mass	Number	Mass
1		13		25	
2		14		26	
3		15		27	
4		16		28	
5		17		29	
6		18		30	
7		19		31	
8		20		32	
9		21		33	
10		22		34	
11		23		35	
12		24		36	

2. Add the mass for each new apple to your line plot. Be careful not to replot your original 12 apples. Before beginning, you might want to check off the numbers for apples you have already placed on the graph.

   There should be _____36_____ points on your line plot. Are there?

3. Is the range for all 36 apples different from the range of your original 12 apples? Explain. Use a separate piece of paper if you need to.

   Answers will vary, but range for the 36 points is most likely to be larger.

The line plots will vary, but the range should include all the data and the intervals should be of equal size.

STUDENT SHEET 1.3 (cont'd)

4. All these apples are considered the same size. Do you think they are the same size? Explain.
Answers will vary, but the discussion should include mention of average size.

5. Do you think that there exists an apple in this variety and size category that has a mass 20 grams less than your smallest apple or 20 grams more than your largest apple? Why, or why not?
Answers will vary, as will rationale.

6. According to the data for all 36 apples, the size ____ *Answers will vary.*
                                                    (variety)
apple has a mass between ____ and ____ grams.
                        (#)

7. A line plot often emphasizes features of the data that were not apparent from the list. These include:

   Outliers: Data values that are very much larger or smaller than the other values.
   Clusters: Isolated groups of points.
   Gaps: Large spaces between points.

   a. The masses of which apples, if any, appear to be outliers?
   Answers will vary.

   b. Do the data seem to fall into clusters on the line plot? If so, where?
   Answers will vary.

   c. Are there any gaps in the data? If so, where?
   Answers will vary.

STUDENT SHEET 1.3 (cont'd)

8. The median mass is the mass exactly in the middle of the range.

   a. Use your line plot to find the median apple mass for your variety of apple.
   Answers will vary.

   b. Describe how you determined the median mass.
   Answers will vary.

9. What percent of your apples have a mass less than the median mass?
   Answers will vary.

10. What percent have a mass more than the median mass? *Answers will vary.*

11. Write a brief description of the information displayed in the line plot.
    Answers will vary, but the discussion should include mention of range, median, clusters, gaps, and outliers.

STUDENT SHEET 1.5 (cont'd)

4. The size _Answers will vary._ apple has a mass between _____ and _____
   (variety)
   _____ grams.
   (#)

5. Are there any outliers in the data? If so, where?
   Answers will vary.

6. Does the data seem to fall into clusters on the line plot? If so, where?
   Answers will vary.

7. Are there any gaps in the data? If so, where?
   Answers will vary.

8. Calculate the median apple mass for this variety of apple.
   Answers will vary.

9. How does the median mass of these apples compare to the median mass of the two other varieties? Explain.
   Answers will vary, but the discussion should include comparison of ranges and medians.

STUDENT SHEET 1.4 (cont'd)

4. The size _Answers will vary._ apple has a mass between _____ and _____
   (variety)
   _____ grams.
   (#)

5. Are there any outliers in the data? If so, where?
   Answers will vary.

6. Does the data seem to fall into clusters on the line plot? If so, where?
   Answers will vary.

7. Are there any gaps in the data? If so, where?
   Answers will vary.

8. Calculate the median mass for this variety of apple.
   Answers will vary.

9. How does the median mass of these apples compare to the median mass of the first variety? Explain.
   Answers will vary, but the discussion should include comparison of range, medians, etc.

7. Are the whiskers equal in length? If not, what does this mean?

Answers will vary, but they should include some mention of the range and/or the extremes as well as the fact that the distribution might not be uniform across the range.

8. Is the median in the center of the box? Why, or why not?

Answers will vary, but the rationale should be consistent with the observation. If the median is not in the center of the box, this means the distribution is not uniform within the IQR.

9. What are the advantages and disadvantages of using a box plot compared to a line or stem plot?

Answers will vary, but there should be mention that the box plot clearly identifies the central point and the range.

The stem plots will vary, but the stem should cover the entire range of the data.

STUDENT SHEET 4.1

Measuring Apples

1. My group is collecting data on the heights and diameters of size _____ (#)

   Answers will vary. apples.
   (variety of apple)

2. My group is measuring the same apples that we found the masses of, apples numbered:

   A. 1–12   B. 13–24   C. 25–36

3. Collect the data by following the directions below:

   a. Some people should measure the height of each apple, and others should measure the diameter. Decide who will measure what.

   b. Use a knife to carefully cut each apple in half vertically. Be sure to label both halves with the same number.

   c. Measure the height and the diameter of each of your 12 apples to the nearest millimeter and record the result in the table on the following page.

4. Should you measure both halves of the same apple? Explain.

   Answers will vary, but they could include some reference to variation in size and/or error in measurement.

5. Using masking tape, label each apple as to variety. Following directions from your teacher, package the apples in plastic bags. The packaging should result in 36 bags, each bag containing three half apples, one half of each variety.

STUDENT SHEET 3.3 (cont'd)

5. On separate paper, write a paragraph giving an overall summary of the three box plots. Describe how the mass of your apples compare to the mass of other varieties in the class. _Answers will vary._

6. Who might be interested in this information? Why?

   Answers will vary, but "apple growers" and "grocery store owners" are possible responses.

7. What kind of predictions can you make based on your interpretations?

   Answers will vary, but should relate to size.

8. What additional data might you collect in order to verify or disprove your conclusions?

   Answers will vary.

Different Displays

Your group is going to display the height and diameter data for all 36 apples in two more modes—stem-and-leaf plots and box plots. Some members of the group should make the plots for the height, and others should make the plots for the diameter. Decide who will make which plots.

Stem Plot

1. Prepare a stem plot of your data.

2. What conclusions can you make by looking at the stem plot you just constructed?

Answers will vary, but students might respond that the data is too clustered to really tell you much.

3. If there are too many leaves per stem, spread out the stem plot as shown and reorganize it.

```
6 | 2 2 4     Put the leaves for 0, 1, 2, 3, and 4 on the first line for each
* | 5 6       stem and the leaves 5, 6, 7, 8, and 9 on the second line.
7 |
* |
```

4. Which of the two stem plots do you think displays the data best? Why?

Answers will vary depending on the spread of the initial distribution.

Box Plot Display

5. Use either of your stem plots to locate the five important values necessary for making a box plot.

median *Answers will vary.*

lower quartile *Answers will vary.*   lower extreme *Answers will vary.*

upper quartile *Answers will vary.*   upper extreme *Answers will vary.*

Displaying Apples

Line Plot for 12 Apples

1. The range of the *Answers will vary.* for these 12 apples is between _____ and _____ mm.

2. Prepare a line plot of your data with a one millimeter interval.

3. Describe the distribution of your data, including discussion of clusters, gaps, outliers, and location of the median.

Answers will vary.

4. Do you feel confident about your observations based on the size of your sample? Explain.

Answers will vary. This response will most likely be a reflection of that to question 3 on Student Sheet 1.3.

Line Plot for 36 Apples

5. Complete the table on Student Sheet 4.1 by collecting the remaining data from your classmates.

6. Add the new data for *Answers will vary.* to your line plot.

7. Describe the distribution of the larger sample. *Answers will vary.*

8. Did enlarging the sample size affect the distribution? Explain.

Answers will vary, but from our experience, the additional data are quite likely not to change the distribution.

3. Your group is going to make two different scatter plots; height versus mass, and diameter versus mass. Decide who in your group will work on which plot.

4. For each scatter plot, set up the grid on Student Sheet 5.2 with the height or diameter on the horizontal axis and the mass on the vertical axis. Label each axis, including the units. Construct each scatter plot by graphing the (H,M) or the (D,M) coordinate pair for each apple.

5. Describe the scatter plot you made.

   Answers will vary, but the discussion should include some mention of the relation between the two.

6. Do you think there is a relation between the two variables in the scatter plot? Explain.

   Answers will vary, but they should be consistent with the scatter plot.

---

6. Determine the interquartile range.
   Answers will vary.

7. Prepare a box plot representing your data with an interval of one millimeter.

8. What does the location of the median tell you about the data?

   The median gives you the central location of the distribution, 50% of data is above the median, and 50% is below.

Summary

9. On a separate sheet of paper, write a paragraph describing what you have learned from studying all three types of plots. Discuss the advantages and disadvantages of each type of display.

   Answers will vary, but they might include reference to the fact that both line plots and stem plots show the shape of the data and the general distribution, including clusters, gaps, and outliers. While the detailed distribution is masked by a box plot, it does highlight critical points, such as the median and quartiles. Both stem plots and box plots are convenient methods for comparing like data.

10. With your group, using the six displays for height and diameter, discuss how you would compare the height to the diameter for your apple variety. Write a brief summary of the process.

    Answers will vary.

11. With your group, use the three displays for height or the three for diameter to discuss how you would compare the heights or diameters of your apples to the other varieties. Be prepared to describe your process to the class.

    Answers will vary.

12. Your data is for size _____ apples. How do you think the size of
    an apple is determined?   (#)

    Answers will vary, but reference might be made to height or diameter.

FAMILY ACTIVITY SHEET 1

Family Taste Test

Materials You Will Need

- The Family Activity taste-test package of apples
- A kitchen paring knife
- 3 plates, one for each variety of apple
- Survey slips, 3 for each family member—1 for each variety of apple
- Scissors
- Pencil or pen
- Family Activity Sheet 3

Getting Ready

Follow the directions given below for each variety of apples separately. Remove the variety label from each apple half. Put one label on or near the plate on which you will place the slices of this variety. Wash the apples with soap and water. Rinse well in cold water. Using a paring knife, take a slice off the exposed part of the apple and discard it. Slice the apple halves into a sufficient number of pieces to allow each family member to have a piece to taste. Place all the slices on a plate.

After washing the paring knife, repeat this process for the other two varieties.

Cut Family Activity Sheets 2 into individual survey slips. You need 3 survey slips for each family member.

Conducting the Taste Test

1. Describe in detail the process that you will use to conduct your family taste-test survey. Use a separate sheet of paper.

   This should reflect the procedure agreed upon by the class.

2. Discuss the project with each person you are surveying and conduct the apple taste test.

3. When everyone has completed the taste test on all three varieties of apples, complete Family Activity Sheet 3.

FAMILY ACTIVITY SHEET 2

Survey Slips

Answers will vary, but one possible response is shown.

Rome Beauty
(variety)

Describe the Flavor and Texture:

Rate the Taste

			x	
1	2	3	4	5
Very Bad	Bad	Okay	Good	Very Good

(variety)

Describe the Flavor and Texture:

Rate the Taste

1	2	3	4	5
Very Bad	Bad	Okay	Good	Very Good

(variety)

Describe the Flavor and Texture:

Rate the Taste

1	2	3	4	5
Very Bad	Bad	Okay	Good	Very Good

(variety)

Describe the Flavor and Texture:

Rate the Taste

1	2	3	4	5
Very Bad	Bad	Okay	Good	Very Good

(variety)

Describe the Flavor and Texture:

Rate the Taste

1	2	3	4	5
Very Bad	Bad	Okay	Good	Very Good

FAMILY ACTIVITY SHEET 3

Family Responses

1. Use the table below to organize your family data. List the ratings for each family member for each variety. It will facilitate the work in class if you group the responses by variety rather than family member. For example, list all the responses to one type of apple before you list any responses to the next type.

Family Taste-Test Ratings   *Answers will vary. A possible response is given.*

Variety	Name	Taste Rating	Texture Description
Granny Smith	*Leroy Jones*	*4*	*tart, crunchy*
Rome Beauty	*Leroy Jones*	*3*	*sweet, crisp*
Red Delicious	*Leroy Jones*	*5*	*very sweet, mushy*
Granny Smith	*Kim Jones*	*5*	*tart, crisp*
Rome Beauty	*Kim Jones*	*4*	*sweet, crisp*
Red Delicious	*Kim Jones*	*2*	*bland, mushy*

2. Did anything surprise you about your results? If so, explain.

Answers will vary.

3. With your family, write a brief summary of your taste-test results.

Answers will vary.

4. Take this sheet and all the completed survey slips to class tomorrow.

FAMILY ACTIVITY SHEET 5

Apple Taste-Test Ratings   *Answers will vary, but a possible response is given.*

Family Name	Granny Smith (variety)	Rome Beauty (variety)	Red Delicious (variety)
1. *Jones*	*4,5*	*3,4*	*5,2*
2.			
3.			
4.			
5.			
6.			
7.			
8.			
9.			
10.			
11.			
12.			
13.			
14.			
15.			
16.			
17.			
18.			
19.			
20.			
21.			
22.			
23.			
24.			
25.			
26.			
27.			
28.			
29.			
30.			